SEEDS FOR DEMOCRATIC FUTURES

Edited by Frederic Hanusch
and Anna Katsman

THE NEW | Volume 2

THE NEW publishes collaborative research in the humanities and social sciences. Its publications offer future-oriented responses to the nested crises of the present along the dimensions of what it means to be human, how to improve democratic self-governance, and how to achieve socio-economic transformation. Our goal is to make humanistic research relevant and accessible to wider audiences.

SEEDS FOR DEMOCRATIC FUTURES

Edited by Frederic Hanusch
and Anna Katsman

THE NEW INSTITUTE   [transcript]

Bibliographic information published by the Deutsche Nationalbibliothek

The Deutsche Nationalbibliothek lists this publication in the Deutsche Nationalbibliografie; detailed bibliographic data are available in the Internet at https://dnb.dnb.de

This work is licensed under the Creative Commons Attribution-ShareAlike 4.0 (BY-SA) which means that the text may be remixed, built upon and be distributed, provided credit is given to the author and that copies or adaptations of the work are released under the same or similar license. For details go to https://creativecommons.org/licenses/by-sa/4.0/

Creative Commons license terms for re-use do not apply to any content (such as graphs, figures, photos, excerpts, etc.) not original to the Open Access publication and further permission may be required from the rights holder. The obligation to research and clear permission lies solely with the party re-using the material.

First published in 2024 by transcript Verlag, Bielefeld
© Frederic Hanusch and Anna Katsman (eds.) and the authors

Cover Design & Typesetting: Maciej Kodzis, CDLX GmbH and THE NEW INSTITUTE

Collages: Mac Premo

Managing Editor: Diana Perry Schnelle

Printed by: Friedrich Pustet GmbH & Co. KG, Regensburg

Print-ISBN 978-3-8376-6943-5
PDF-ISBN 978-3-8394-6943-9
EPUB-ISBN 978-3-7328-6943-5

https://doi.org/10.14361/9783839469439

ISSN of series: 2510-9286
eISSN of series: 2510-9294

Printed on permanent acid-free text paper.

| | Introduction | Sowing Seeds of Democracy | 9 |
| | | Frederic Hanusch and Anna Katsman | |

I   Seeds for Reorientation

- **Not Hope, but Faith** — Ece Temelkuran — 23
- **Compassionate Governance and Attaining Flourishing in Democracy** — Andrej Zwitter — 29
- **Democracy Between Plural Knowledge Systems** — Madhulika Banerjee — 39
- **Intersections & Interventions: Black Feminism in the Age of the Polycrisis** — Minna Salami — 49
- **From Climate Coloniality to Pluriversalizing Democracy** — Tobias Müller — 57
- **Sustainable Development Cannot be the Future We Want** — Louis J. Kotzé — 71

II   Seeds for Repair

- **Tackling Discoursive Polarization: Welcome Radical Ideas but not Aggression!** — Michael Brüggemann — 87
- **Universities as Truthsayers** — John Aubrey Douglass — 99
- **Socialization as a Counter-Right to Democratize and Reclaim the Common** — Isabel Feichtner — 113

		Dethroning Elections: Why the Future of Democracy Requires New Ways of Picking Leaders Max Krahé	123
		Instructing our Representatives: An Argument in Favor of the Imperative Mandate Bruno Leipold	133
III	Seeds for the New	Generative AI and Democracy Judith Simon	145
		Experimental Democracy for the Digital Age Rahel Süß	155
		Planetary Democracy: Towards Radical Inclusivity Frederic Hanusch	167
		Incorporating Futures into Democracy: Imagining More Maki Sato	177
		An Art of Association: Democracy and Dance Anna Katsman	187
		Think Future, Act Present: Dreams of Creative Democracies László Upor	193

About the Authors	203
About the Illustrations	205
Acknowledgments	207

INTRODUCTION

SOWING SEEDS OF DEMOCRACY

FREDERIC HANUSCH AND ANNA KATSMAN

As we navigate a changing world marked by rapid technological advancements, political radicalization, growing geopolitical hostilities, and a planet on fire, one might easily forget the value, power, and beauty of democracy with its capacity for renewal. Yet, periods of profound change carry deep ambivalence as they hold both the potential for democratizing democracy and the risk of it crumbling under the weight of these changes. In this time of great unsettledness, the future of democracy hangs precariously in the balance: in 2023, democracy declined in 42 countries (V-Dem Institute, 2024). As the pillars of democracy — ranging from the freedom of expression, the integrity of elections, the rule of law, to the protection of civil liberties — are eroding, this book aims to sow seeds that can help reclaim, reinforce, and complement these vital elements in the face of modern autocratization.

Among all known political forms, democracy has the best chance of steering technologies to work for the public good, uniting democratic-minded people of all kinds, and keeping the planet habitable. The urgency of contemporary problems calls on us not to sideline democracy as less important than the "real issues," but instead to reevaluate its essence, to embrace its spirit anew, and to reinvigorate the very foundations upon which democratic societies thrive. Without fundamental changes to the way it is practiced, the democratic way of life will not be able to continue in the wake of the transformations to come.

Building on this observation as a starting point, the analyses and respective proposals in this book aim to demonstrate that democracies are hampered in responding to the challenges of the present not in virtue of being democratic, but rather because they are not democratic *enough*. We thus attempt to present some ideas on how to possibly revive democracies, and how to develop democratic counter-narratives, accompanying recent analyses that have profoundly shown us "how democracies die" (Levitsky and Ziblatt, 2019) or "how democracy ends" (Runciman, 2018).

Of course, a range of approaches already aims to renew democracy, most prominently in the form of democratic innovations that seek to deepen citizen engagement (Elstub and Escobar, 2019; Smith, 2009). They explore ways to engage citizens in political processes and address democratic deficits, often attempting to find solutions for concrete policy problems at hand. This includes such formats as mini-publics, citizen assemblies, participatory budgeting, and deliberative forums. Each of these approaches has its merits, particularly for preconfigured settings. We take a slightly different and rather organic perspective in this book, aiming to encompass approaches that may primarily address the unconfigured democratic spaces.

Each essay in this book sows a democratic seed. Each of these seeds carries the capacity for renewal, just like the DNA resting in a natural seed. This capacity comes from an abundance of knowledge worked out over time, compressed into a packed bundle of possibilities for future flourishing. These seeds thus emerge from existing ecosystems of knowledge as the authors demonstrate. Our proposals aim to open space for academic and practical conversations around ideas that mostly remain at the edges of mainstream discussions of democratic renewal. As with all seeds, some may take root and develop, receiving enough resources and care, while others will not find such hospitable conditions.

Just as a tree must produce many seeds so that a new tree may arise, the future of democracy is in better hands if manifold perspectives on its renewal are offered. We deliberately adopted a multi-perspective approach, embracing heterogeneity to foster a rich dialogue across various forms of knowledge. As Maya Angelou once famously put it: "In diversity there is beauty and there is strength," be it cultural, biological, or democratic diversity. The book comprises this diversity in three sections: seeds for reorientation, seeds for repair, and seeds for the new.

The first section, "Seeds for Reorientation," serves as the foundation, offering ideas that challenge the traditional knowledge underpinning mainstream concepts of democracy. Ece Temelkuran sets the tone by arguing that in these harsh times, what we need is not hope — which she interprets as a paralyzed response to the present — but rather "faith." She suggests that secular faith is more practical and grounded than hope, as it embodies the patience and determination required to do the "thankless work" demanded by our current circumstances.

In his essay "Compassionate Governance and Attaining Flourishing in Democracy," Andrej Zwitter also emphasizes that an emotional shift is necessary for reorienting our democracies. Drawing on Aristotle, he argues that compassion and agape are crucial for recalibrating democratic representation to serve the "most vulnerable, not the most powerful." Zwitter believes that this approach can counter the overly materialistic and rationalist limitations of democracy, paving the way for both individual and collective flourishing.

Madhulika Banerjee's essay "Democracy Between Plural Knowledge Systems" provides a path for reorientation in this regard, investigating the planetary crisis in the context of modern production systems and their impact on the environment. She emphasizes the need to acknowledge and integrate non-modern knowledge systems, which historically operated with a deep respect for the planet. These knowledges could offer potential solutions to the planetary crisis by revitalizing local, diverse, and democratic production practices. She therefore suggests the democratization of the relationship between scientific and non-modern knowledge.

Minna Salami calls for a turn to sensuous knowledge in her essay "Intersections & Interventions: Black Feminism in the Age of the Polycrisis." She draws parallels between the intersecting oppressions faced by Black women and the multiple crises confronting our planet. On the basis of these parallels, she introduces the transformative potential of

Black feminist thought to reshape our understanding of reality, power dynamics, and agency. Central here is the role of embodied knowledge, expressed through poetry, music, and the arts, in providing a deeper understanding of the present and its challenges.

While it is important to recognize that new forms of colonialism are currently evolving, such as China's approach to its neighboring states and particularly in Africa, it is equally important to understand how previous forms of colonialism still impact contemporary societies. Tobias Müller's essay focuses in that regard on the significance of oppressed groups to properly frame a progressive democratic politics. In "From Climate Coloniality to Pluriversalizing Democracy," Müller argues that addressing climate justice requires acknowledging the historical impacts of colonialism and extractivism on society's relationship with the planet. He advocates for a pluriversal approach, rooted in indigenous and feminist knowledge, to tackle climate injustice and prevent further harm to marginalized groups. Müller stresses the importance of a democratic response that challenges Eurocentric norms, extends representation, and supports grassroots movements for planetary repair.

Louis J. Kotzé takes up Müller's call, and in his essay "Sustainable Development Cannot be the Future We Want" challenges the concept of sustainable development, critiquing it as a neoliberal invention that is in conflict with democracy. Kotzé contends that sustainable development is used as a superficial response to the deeper causes of ecological decline. The essay argues that the Sustainable Development Goals (SDGs), despite their ambitious aims, are hindered by their foundation in sustainable development dogma, which fails to provide the radical transformations needed to address the planetary crisis in a democratic manner.

Complementing the broad and idealistic perspectives of the first section, the essays in the second section, "Seeds for Repair," focus on contemporary democratic practices and explore how democracy can be rejuvenated from within. Grounded in the constraints of our present reality, these essays are primarily concerned with revitalizing existing democratic institutions.

In "Tackling Discursive Polarization: Welcome Radical Ideas but not Aggression!," Michael Brüggemann discusses how journalism and digital platforms contribute to discursive polarization within societies, emphasizing the harmful impact of polarized debates on democratic decision-making and societal cohesion. He suggests that media outlets and digital platforms should shift their focus towards highlighting common ground, bridging differences, and featuring constructive voices. He further argues for the adoption of practices such as constructive journalism, solutions-oriented reporting, and algorithmic curation that promote substantive dialogue and depolarization while still allowing space for radical ideas and critical debates. But it is not only journalism and social media platforms that can address harmful polarization and rising autocracy: universities can also play a central role in repairing democracy.

John Aubrey Douglass investigates this power of universities in "Universities as Truthsayers," particularly in the context of rising neo-nationalist movements and autocratic-leaning governments. Douglass focuses on universities in liberal democracies and discusses their potential to combat negative perceptions, engage with local communities, and contribute to socioeconomic prosperity. He emphasizes the importance of universities as sources of truth, knowledge, and rational thinking, suggesting that they should expand their research portfolios, improve communication strategies, and play a vital role in shaping public discourse.

If building common ground is important when it comes to ideological polarization, "commoning" is seen as equally important for repairing a polarized political economy. The underlying analysis, that the wealthy and powerful should not have more to say in a democracy, is key to Isabel Feichtner's essay "Socialization as a Counter-Right to Democratize and Reclaim the Common," in which she explores how law can contribute to a democratic social-ecological transformation. Feichtner discusses transformative law and its connection to social practice, highlighting two promising projects: commoning and socialization. Commoning involves collective self-organization for equitable provisioning and non-destructive value production. The movement to socialize housing in Berlin is investigated as an example of a transformative counter-right, potentially democratizing society through the emergence of a new common.

In "Dethroning Elections: Why the Future of Democracy Requires New Ways of Picking Leaders," Max Krahé argues that elections, which have become synonymous with democracy, can actually undermine democracy's core principles. Krahé contends that elections create a hierarchy by focusing on candidates rather than voters, leading to division and a distinction between leaders and the electorate. He examines the historical shift from sortition (random selection) to elections, driven by arguments for selecting capable rulers and preventing instability, but emphasizes that elections favor the wealthy and foster psychological and societal issues such as apathy, pride, and rage. Krahé suggests that a combination of sortition and experimentation could offer a more genuinely democratic and inclusive alternative to elections.

This critique of representative democracy is shared by Bruno Leipold. In "Instructing our Representatives: An Argument in Favor of the Imperative Mandate," he joins Krahé's call to critically examine representative democracy by highlighting the prevalence of politicians' broken promises and their alignment with corporate interests. Leipold argues that the current understanding of democracy as representative government lacks accountability, since representatives often disregard their constituents' wishes once elected. He discusses the historical concept of the imperative mandate — which emphasizes binding representatives to the instructions of their constituents — and suggests various ways to implement it, such as Constituency Assemblies.

The third section, "Seeds for the New," deals with emerging phenomena for which no blueprints for democratizing exist. This section offers unconventional ideas that may add to, substantially alter, or even break away from existing democratic practices and institutions.

Without a doubt, this kind of new phenomenon is embodied in the recent expansive usage of large language models (LLMs). In "Generative AI and Democracy," Judith Simon examines the rapid rise of Generative AI and its implications for democracy. She discusses the capabilities of Generative AI to produce high-quality text, images, and videos, highlighting its potential for deception and manipulation. The problems of deception are categorized into four aspects: deception about human interaction, deception about AI capabilities, deceptive results generated by AI, and deception as the result of integrating AI into other services and products. Simon emphasizes the need for a multi-faceted approach involving legal, technical, and other measures to address the challenges posed by Generative AI, including labeling content, promoting transparency, and fostering education that encompasses an understanding of AI's impact on society.

Avoiding the danger and using the advantages is also what Rahel Süß argues for in her essay "Experimental Democracy for the Digital Age." She discusses the impact of predictive technologies on democracy, highlighting the risks of pre-emptive strategies and the loss of an open future. She proposes a model of experimental democracy as a way to renew democracy in the digital era. The model aims to empower citizens in shaping the digital future by shifting power, building sustainable digital communities, and opening up opportunities for experimentation. Süß suggests using technology to challenge, build, and scale power, focusing on community experiences and inclusivity, ultimately aiming for a future-opening democracy organized around the principles of plurality and conflict.

Novel technologies are also a prerequisite for what Frederic Hanusch calls a "planetary democracy." In his essay "Planetary Democracy: Towards Radical Inclusivity," Hanusch argues for a shift in the concept of democracy to incorporate the planet and its interconnected forces. The need for radical inclusivity of both human and non-human is discussed, drawing parallels to historical struggles for civil rights and representation of marginalized groups. The establishment of planetary democracy involves recognizing non-human entities' interests, utilizing advanced technologies like sensors and machine learning to communicate with them, and experimenting with new democratic institutions that encompass more-than-human agencies to keep the Earth habitable.

Such an account goes well beyond currently established anthropocentric democracies, requiring imagination, which is at the center of Maki Sato's essay "Incorporating Futures into Democracy: Imagining More." In this essay she challenges the limitations of conventional future predictions based on past trends and numerical modeling, proposing an approach that embraces creativity. Sato discusses the necessity of considering the perspectives of future generations, non-human entities, and the planetary commons in decision-making. The concept of an "imagined community" is expanded over time to create a sense of belonging to a shared ideal future, prompting citizens to collaboratively design and backcast from that vision.

Even though such imagination is targeted at the far future, it is based in the here and now, within and through our existing bodies; a circumstance that requires greater attention as Anna Katsman not only envisions but enables us to experience in her essay "An Art of Association:

Democracy and Dance." She presents the concept of contact improvisation as a practice that fosters democratic values through physical interaction and collaboration. The practice involves entering a space with others and engaging in movement based on mutual sensing, trust-building, and shared agency. Through non-verbal communication and responsiveness, participants create a dynamic environment that mirrors democratic principles of mutual respect, cooperation, and equal participation, challenging conventional structures of democracy and fostering an embodied sense of togetherness.

Lastly, László Upor's essay on "Think Future, Act Present: Dreams of Creative Democracies" emphasizes the importance of social movements as transformative agents in repairing and revitalizing democracies. Upor therefore draws parallels between the interconnectedness of the human body and society, asserting that social movements are vital to repairing and regenerating the sensitive fabric of democracy. He highlights the power of collective action in raising awareness, creating community, and effecting change, while also emphasizing the need for adaptability, imagination, and collaboration to address the complex challenges facing societies today. After all, this is a call to action for everyone to practice democracy anew.

Understanding and enacting democratization in the sense advocated for by these seeds means that varying approaches can and should exist next to one another: the more diverse the democratic fabrics become, the more resilient they are. Again, not all seeds will take root. Some of the essays are meant more as provocations for thought and experimentation, rather than proposals for direct implementation. The aim is to stimulate thought and practice around these issues. Only through the democratic process of testing these ideas in a public space will it become clearer which will take off. And as uncertainty is constitutive for democratic futures, different approaches must be tried, without aiming for a master approach that outcompetes all other approaches. Just as seeds become plants, the essays in this collection also form an ecosystem that is closely connected, composed of interacting parts. In most cases, the approaches nurture rather than harm each other, such as sustainable digital democracy enabling planetary democracy and vice versa. Yet in other cases, we might find rivalries when, for example, the recognition of climate coloniality demands even more fundamental changes than a comprehensive reform of existing representative and electoral democracies.

Quick fixes and one-size-fits-all solutions rarely succeed in the complex task of democratizing democracies. Instead, the emergence of new democratic practices is promising when these practices are curated and tailored to the histories and aspirations of a society. Our approach is thus closely aligned to what Albert Hirschman named possibilism: "an approach to the social world that would stress the unique rather than the general, the unexpected rather than the expected, and the possible rather than the probable" (Hirschman 1971, p. 28). In that respect, this book is an invitation. May these essays ignite debate, inspire us to transcend the confines of pessimism and complacency, and motivate us to cultivate seeds of democratic futures in our daily lives and beyond.[1]

---

1   This book grew out of conversations among fellows at THE NEW INSTITUTE in 2022–23, most of whom were part of "The Future of Democracy" program.

References

Elstub, S., & Escobar, O. (2019). *Handbook of Democratic Innovation and Governance*. Oxford University Press.

Hirschman, A. O. (1971). *A Bias for Hope: Essays on Development and Latin America*. Yale University Press.

Levitsky, S., & Ziblatt, D. (2019). *How Democracies Die*. Crown.

Runciman, D. (2018). *How Democracy Ends*. Profile Books.

Smith, G. (2009). *Democratic Innovations: Designing Institutions for Citizen Participation*. Cambridge University Press.

V-Dem Institute. (2024). *Democracy Report*. https://v-dem.net/documents/44/v-dem_dr2024_highres.pdf

I

SEEDS FOR REORIENTATION

NOT HOPE, BUT FAITH

ECE TEMELKURAN

Revolution is a word made of blood. It is history's most exquisite daemon asking for human sacrifice. Perhaps that is why throughout human history the term is pronounced more carelessly by the young, those clueless both about death and the consuming ordinariness of a long life. It is the crazy diamond.

It is the sweetest word, however. Like love and rage, lust and dignity, it electrifies a nerve in humans that turns the ordinary man into David. The word induces the illusion of being bigger and stronger than we actually are and makes us so. Revolution, even one mention of it in a loud voice, immediately builds a universe of emotions where there is no tomorrow, gifting us with the ultimate liberation from all fear and every drop of existential boredom. A giant whirlpool fans out everything that is not pure enough for the zenith of human existence and concentrates an iron seed of togetherness in joy for the many. Yet, revolution — as has been repeatedly proven in modern history — is a hungry beast that eats the most beautiful among us, leaving behind the mediocre to rule the ruins of our dream of building heaven on earth. And in today's world, it is nearly impossible to convince people of the possibility of a utopia when the ticking of the countdown to the physical demise of the planet is so loud. Thus, we need a better word for our times — a new *pathos* that is less bloodthirsty and more reasonable.

Today, there is political inertia that is curiously disproportionate in the face of the urgent polycrisis our globe is experiencing. Yet, funnily enough, there are plenty of ideas for what to do to reverse the dangerous current of history. There is enough potential political energy waiting to be transformed into kinetic energy. There is enough rage, pain, and indignity to be mobilized. Unfortunately, however, lethargy is more present than it was a few decades ago. And as a code for the curious silence, a ghost word hovers over our political debates and the wide-ranging worrying topics, from climate catastrophe to the crisis of capitalism. The word hope, with its soft hands, has been abducting every conversation worldwide for the last decade. There is a reoccurring, almost tiring demand for hope. And to understand the reason for the current political lethargy, we should look more closely into the word hope and the insistent demand for it. Because only when we reveal the angel-faced perniciousness of hope can we enlarge our lexicon of politics and find a better term, or rather a pathos, to replace the word revolution. And maybe then we might even have sufficient stamina to work towards the dogma, that big idea to follow to change the world, the system.

"Is there hope?" It's a question I've been asked countless times in several languages in numerous countries. After writing a book demonstrating that rising rightwing populism is a global phenomenon, and that a new form of fascism is a natural and consistent consequence of the neoliberal politics of the last five decades, when the audiences were convinced enough that full-force fascism is a close-by political possibility, this question of hope landed at the end of every talk I gave. Every time a member of the audience voiced it, the texture of the silence in the room became a lead-like substance, even though the word hope is supposed to induce a feather-like sense of lightness. The heaviness caused by the mention of the word meant only one thing: Hope calls for hopelessness louder than any other word. It is declared only because its antonym is more present and dominant than itself. However, the word and its presence in political conversation have several different and critical repercussions.

Hope is too fragile a word for our harsh times. If the term describing the central struggle in our age is survival — and it is — then the word hope is not only useless but also irrelevant. Survival is the mode of existence where a person never asks for hope and just keeps going. For those trying to survive, life is built on words such as *nevertheless*, *despite*, and *against all odds*. The person can spare no time convincing himself to continue the struggle for survival, he just survives. With a certain emotional numbness, he does the things required to be alive and remain standing. Imagine a miner under the rubble trying to dig out of the debris with his hands despite not seeing a single ray of light. Picture a refugee who is certain that he'll be sent back once he reaches the shore yet swims towards the land nevertheless, or a Covid patient trying to inhale just one more time, against all odds. None of us is any different than the miner or the refugee — as the human species, we are on the verge of extinction, politically and otherwise. Our daily comforts and the general nitty-gritty of life are distracting enough to make us forget the dire reality, yet this is where humanity stands today. Asking for hope or demanding proof of its existence is not only a waste of time but also reduces the strength dedicated to our struggle for survival.

Hope is too inconsequential a concept to be a component of political thinking. And the way to prove this is whenever the question of hope arises, to respond "What if there is hope? What would it change in your political actions tomorrow?" Or even better: "What if there is no hope? What would you be doing differently tomorrow?" The silence you get as the answer to these two questions is enough evidence that the question of hope does nothing but paralyze the political conversation by steering it into a cul-de-sac. In that endless cul-de-sac are the fake prophets of hope, enslaving the masses with their need for hope to act, and people who are woolgathering long enough to dismiss their initial and inherent political agency.

Having said all this, one should not be so cruel as to disregard the hopelessness of the masses. It is needless to deny that we all feel like the meek villagers terrified by the Goliath of the polycrisis. As the prize-winning movie of 2022 proclaimed, "Everything Everywhere All at Once." Unless we are too immersed in political work to busy ourselves with procrastination, the depth and the scale of the polycrisis leave us with two options: to develop numbness or to be overwhelmed. Both states of mind are impenetrable for fragile words such as hope. Thus, we need a sharp and mighty word with which to arm ourselves. That word is faith — faith in humankind and in politics. Hope is a placeholder term for the concept of a reason. When people ask for hope, they ask for a reason to get up and fight back against Goliath. And this is because our "raison d'être" for political action was stolen from us approximately five decades ago when the slogan "There is no alternative" (TINA) took center stage. "There is no alternative," declared a woman with an Asprey bag and an old cowboy with American glee.[1] On both sides of the Atlantic, the rulers of global politics and finance ordered the people of the world to give up their political agency, in exchange for free markets and capitalist globalization. Even though the order was implemented through brutality and oppression, in the end it was so successful that two generations have grown up being convinced that politics is too dirty to be involved in, the economy is too complex to be handled by politics, and there is no longer the need to think beyond the current system. That was when, without knowing it, the majority pledged to believe in the neoliberal definition of a human — a self-centered, selfish, competitive, bastardly being that doesn't deserve to be loved or sacrificed for through political action. That's how we lost our faith in humans, the ugly beings. And that's when we lost our inherent desire for politics, our raison d'être for political action — which, until then, had been the blind faith of humankind accompanied by the elation of doing politics with and for them. Thus, today's maddening political lethargy and the sheepish masses constantly asking the wrong question, asking about hope.

Faith — secular faith in humankind and politics — fits the needs of our times, for it, more than any other word, consists of words such as *nevertheless*, *nonetheless*, and *despite*. It signifies the magic ability of our kind that gives us that much-needed *conviction* — as Yeats once put it — to do the consuming and thankless work the current political state of the world calls for. When the world doesn't need a revolution but rather a transformation, what we need is determined patience, a maddening level of forgiveness, and the stubbornness of an evangelical.

1   I am, of course, referring to the politicians Margaret Thatcher and Ronald Reagan.

Transformation, a word that cannot promise us the handsome heroes that revolutions do, nor does it give us the hype of the all-out rebellion, in fact asks much more from us than a revolution does. It is the least bloodthirsty tool capable of changing the world into a more humane place. However, the struggle — the blood, sweat, and tears — that it calls for is no less than the revolution. The courage it requires has to be more sustainable, and the conviction it needs is far more formidable. Because the emotional stamina required for one to keep one's moral and political spine straight is present abundantly in a revolution. In contrast, the transformation depends on one's faith in the journey despite the impossibility of the destination.

Faith is a moral and political stance that needs no proof. It needs miracles. Faith is a relentless force that knows no surrender and never steps back. It gives us the pathos that is lacking in each of us, thanks to the deeply engrained cynicism of our times, which makes us terrified of looking naive. It is the force we need when people are no longer moved by or even interested in facts. Faith is the source of strength that enables us to sacrifice our lives to change the world, providing us with the scarcest mineral in today's world: meaning. By doing so, it connects us, once again, to the undamaged definition of the human, a creature that cannot live without meaning. An animal that is intrinsically inclined to sacrifice itself to and for meaning.

Once meaning is present, the joy of political action follows — another component of near political history that we were made to forget by being told insistently that we — the ones who had once thrown ourselves into selfless political action for the good of people — were now defeated. The stories of our defeat have been told back to us so many times that we have forgotten the very essence of our political action: the joy of togetherness in the struggle, the mightiness of political friendship, and the wholeness felt when the self becomes one with the mass. And that is the miracle faith calls for. And these are the concepts — joy and the power of togetherness — that we need to discuss repeatedly to reinvent our faith in humankind and political action, not because there will be an ultimate victory at the end, but because we cannot risk the ultimate defeat of the human species.

To integrate such concepts and thinking into our political debate, we need to leave our condescending view of the politics of emotions behind. Considering the fact that the politics of emotions is mastered by the global rightwing populists, we, the anti-fascists, the climate activists, and the defenders of social equality, need to take the fears and the learnt numbness of the masses seriously and create a new lexicon of politics to move the crowds. Only then can we achieve the largest togetherness that the Goliath of the polycrisis demands from us. Only then can we find in ourselves the power to do the massive work to mend democracy, which has become mere theatrics of itself without any social justice. Then maybe we can once again talk about faith in democracy and find the faithful who will fight to preserve it.

COMPASSIONATE GOVERNANCE AND ATTAINING FLOURISHING IN DEMOCRACY

ANDREJ ZWITTER

We commonly believe that the best political system invented so far is democracy. There is a lot of evidence in favor of this assumption and political theory has struggled to come up with political systems that are better suited to ensuring the individual's autonomy while organizing collective decision-making. While the conception of democracy seems to be rationally coherent, the political system must be able to address forces outside that of reason. Notably, Hans Morgenthau described politics as the art of managing the inherent human drive of the *animus dominandi* (the will to dominate or subjugate others) — a drive that, unlike rational greed, inherently seeks to dominate others by diminishing them. This destructive force evades reason and requires, in Morgenthau's view, specific attention. He argues that if politics is inherently evil, as it requires the *animus dominandi* for its functioning in political representation, then political science and statecraft is the art of the smallest evil for the greatest good (Morgenthau, 1945). By extension, there is a parallel between Morgenthau's argument and Reinhold Niebuhr's plaidoyer on the limits of reason to design a compassionate system of governance against the immoral impulses of society (Niebuhr, 1932/2013). While Morgenthau highlights the inherent drive for domination in politics, I propose that such tendencies can be mitigated through a framework of compassionate governance. This approach integrates moral and emotive (emotional and moving) imperatives into normative structures in the hope of ensuring that democratic systems not only represent the majority but actively work towards the flourishing of all. If reason cannot be the sole determinant of good governance, as both Morgenthau and Niebuhr argue, then how can we guarantee that individual moral impetus — rather than the individual's desire to dominate others — becomes relevant in democratic governance? This question lies at the core of compassionate governance.

This essay argues that true flourishing, as envisioned by Aristotle's *eudaimonia*, can only be achieved through compassionate governance — a system where the emotional and moral imperatives of agape[1] and compassion recalibrate democratic representation to prioritize the well-being of the least enfranchised members of society. The overall argument of this contribution is that in order to foster individual and collective flourishing, a governance system of democratic justice based on reason might not suffice. Instead, the emotive aspects of *agape* and compassion might serve as non-materialist and non-rationalist foundations to recalibrate representation in the sense of a structural normative solution rather than a political discursive one. From this perspective, democratic representation would not be based on identity but on compassion for the destitute and disenfranchised. I will first discuss flourishing as conceptualized by Aristotle for political governance (section 1). Next, I will use Niebuhr's thoughts on collective immoral impulses in democratic governance to illuminate the limits that democracy can impose on fostering flourishing for all its citizens, including the poor and disenfranchised (section 2). Finally, I will propose a model of governance that puts *agape* and compassion — rather than identity — at the center of democratic representation.

1   Agape in this philosophical framework transcends individual emotions and attachments, embodying a moral and ethical commitment to the flourishing of all members of the community. It is a guiding principle that motivates individuals and leaders to act with compassion and empathy, prioritizing the needs and dignity of the least enfranchised members of society.

I. How Can We Attain Human Flourishing in Democracy?

In his introduction to *Politics*, Aristotle explains that his work on politics should be seen as an extension of his treatment of ethics. In this line of reasoning, Aristotle expands on his ideas about virtues as an individual and collective manifestation in which:

> [...] if the end is the same for an individual and for a city-state, that of the city-state seems at any rate greater and more complete to attain and preserve. For although it is worthy to attain it for only an individual, it is nobler and more divine to do so for a nation or city-state. (Nicomachean Ethics, I.2.1094b7–10)

In other words, if ethics — and particularly virtue ethics as conceptualized by the Socratic school — is the art of flourishing and attaining happiness as an individual, politics should be viewed as the art of collective flourishing and the ability of the statesman to attain individual and collective flourishing (or *eudaimonia*, see below) within the right political system.

In his *Nicomachean Ethics* and *Historia Animalium*, Aristotle reiterates his classification of human beings as political animals (amongst the bees, wasps, ants, and cranes), partly gregarious, partly solitary. It is, therefore, impossible for humans to thrive without solitary contemplation (the solitary aspect of human nature); but neither are they capable of flourishing outside of a community in which they can exercise social virtue. In fact, Aristotle argues, the basic purpose of communities is to promote human flourishing, and he defines the highest human good as *eudaimonia*, which is often translated as "happiness" or "flourishing." However, *eudaimonia* does not consist of a state of mind or a feeling of pleasure or contentment. Instead, it is an activity of the soul in accordance with virtue. Amongst the virtues, Aristotle identified *phronesis* or "wisdom" as the virtue that moderates all other virtues and is responsible for knowing which virtue should apply and to what extent in any given situation. Therefore, according to Aristotle, *eudaimonia* consists of the effective combination of *phronesis* and reason, and human virtue; and excellence in character is that combination of traits or qualities that enables humans to flourish (Mulgan, 1974).

Humans are incapable of flourishing in isolation. They need a community to thrive — a community that they aim to influence to suit their needs: the *polis*. In his *Politics*, Aristotle argues that the goal of the state should be to promote the good life for its citizens, which consists of virtuous activity in accordance with reason. This involves creating laws and institutions that encourage and support virtuous behavior and discourage vice. Aristotle's concept of *eudaimonia*, or flourishing, necessitates a community that promotes virtue. In modern terms, this can be interpreted as a call for governance systems that not only uphold justice and reason but also embed compassion and *agape* in their foundational structural governance principles. Compassionate governance, therefore, becomes essential to achieving the collective flourishing Aristotle envisioned. Aristotle does not go as far as many contemporary political scientists tend to in declaring democracy the superior political system. In Book II of *Politics*, Aristotle discusses the Spartan, the Cretan, and the Carthaginian constitutions. Aristotle views democracy as a deviant constitution, inherently unjust if it assumes property is the qualifying criterion for participation in the *polis*. He does, however, admit that it is the least deviant and unjust system, and that the pooling of wisdom from the crowd leads to a more moral functioning of the political system. And when property is no longer the criterion for participation in the polis, democracy constitutes the only system that is conducive to structural implementation of representational justice based on compassion. Ultimately, according to Aristotle, the role of the state and the statesman is to ensure that the individual can exercise their virtues to attain *eudaimonia* (Miller, 2022). The actual practice of democratic governance, however, has its limitations.

II. Dilemmas Within Political Systems that Must be Overcome

It might be up to the state to ensure flourishing and the well-being of the citizen. The question, however, remains whether governance through the state and by statesmen is indeed the right way to ensure *eudaimonia*.

As Aristotle theorized, there are corrupted forms of each of the governance models: royalty can lead to tyranny under the wrong statesman; aristocracy can lead to oligarchy when the focus moves from the common good of the state to just a part of it; and constitutional democracy can lead to the dictatorship of the many. Morgenthau's depiction of politics as inherently driven by the will to dominate remains problematic in an Aristotelian politics of flourishing. It can be countered by integrating Niebuhr's insights into the moral failures of democratic societies. Arguing in favor of reason as the grounding principle of democratic governance disregards moral, amoral, and immoral individual emotive drives relevant in democratic practice.

When the American Protestant political theologian Niebuhr published his book *Moral Man and Immoral Society* in 1932, it was a response to the injustices he had witnessed in a society proclaiming itself to be democratic and just. This purported justice and morality, supposedly inherent to democracy, was somehow missing. While individuals may act morally, it did not translate to the societal level. Within democratic collective governance, Niebuhr identified a complacency on the part of the majority and those in power to do the right thing for the well-being of those who are disenfranchised. Embedded in and defined by the socio-political system, the sum of certain individuals' actions and decisions will lead to immoral consequences for the destitute and the disenfranchised. Niebuhr saw something in the system of democratic governance that corrupts the translation of the individual moral impetus from the micro level to the macro level. On the collective level, a certain egoism, pride, and hypocrisy unfolds that is not present on the individual level. This might be due to the need to represent collective interests, which is not present on the individual, empathic level. To represent the interests of the group that elected the politician becomes an ethical obligation of the elected individual. This representational political duty, however, causes effects that lead to immoral societies composed of moral people. Aspects of this stem from insecurity and anxious defensiveness of humans in their finiteness, the locale of "original sin" in Niebuhr's perspective. Inspiring the moral sentiments of social classes in a social struggle, according to Niebuhr, relies on dogmas, symbols, and emotionally potent oversimplifications. These lead to a struggle between the dominant ruling class and the subjugated classes. He argues:

> *No class of industrial workers will ever win freedom from the dominant classes if they give themselves completely to the "experimental techniques" of the modern educators. They will have to believe rather more firmly in the justice and in the probable triumph of their cause, than any impartial science would give them the right to believe, if they are to have enough energy to contest the power of the strong. They may be very scientific in projecting their social goal and in choosing the most effective instruments for its attainment, but a motive force will be required to nerve them for their task which is not easily derived from the cool objectivity of science. Modern educators are, like rationalists of all the ages, too enamored of the function of reason in life. The world of history, particularly in man's collective behavior, will never be conquered by reason, unless reason uses tools, and is itself driven by forces which are not rational.*
> (Niebuhr, 2013, pp. xv–xvi)

It is hard to dispute this fundamental critique of the tools of reason in political science in the context of the class struggle between the dominant classes and the subjugated ones in a democracy. The motive — or better emotive (emotional and moving) — force that drives class behavior is derived from symbols, metaphors, and metaphysical principles surrounding the eternal contest of forces. And while the ruling class will argue for peace in favor of perpetuating the status quo (the purported right of all citizens), the struggling class (in Niebuhr's case, industrial workers), who demand justice and a change of system, do not have the system of governance, the executive, legislature, and judiciary on their side. They are left but with one possibility to attain justice, and Niebuhr therefore concludes that this last resort is the use of force to attain equity where peace will not give it to them. Niebuhr's critique of democratic systems points to their failure to translate individual morality into collective justice. Compassionate governance addresses this by embedding moral imperatives into the very structure of governance, ensuring that policies and decisions are driven by a commitment to the well-being of all, especially the disenfranchised.

III. Compassionate Governance: Recalibrating Democratic Representation

Compassionate governance is a framework in which democratic representation is guided by the principles of *agape* and compassion. It structurally requires that those in power prioritize the needs and well-being of the most vulnerable, ensuring that governance is not merely a representation of majority interests but a commitment to the flourishing of all. There is a fundamental incongruence between Aristotle's theory of political governance by methods of reason and what this means in the practice of democratic governance from the perspective of Niebuhr. According to Niebuhr, democracy as a political system that, once established, fosters the establishment of interest groups or classes (some more powerful than others). As designed by democratic governance, it should be in the interest of each of these groups to be in the majority and thus in power. This by design, would consequently result in the suppression of the disenfranchised if they are not represented in the majority. A well-designed welfare state ensures that the disenfranchised never entirely fall through the cracks of general benevolence. However, the same system that ensures their survival also curtails political resistance other than by representation. Together with an economic system that aids those who already have wealth, the liberal economic state built on democracy makes socio-economic mobility and social justice very difficult. Any class struggle that aims to change this representation violates democratic principles, since the ideas and emotive arguments designed to motivate the suppressed are by necessity intolerant of those in power.

There are, it seems, fundamental limitations to designing a rational system of just democratic governance that truly ensures *eudaimonia* for all citizens. What remains overlooked is Aristotle's initial inspiration for a fair political system is that of the promotion of the right virtues. In order to create sufficient conditions for *eudaimonia*, i.e., the practice of virtues and the attainment of flourishing and the well-being of all citizens, it requires a moral aptitude beyond mere abidance by the law. Hence, devising a rational and logical system is not sufficient. This is where compassion and *agape* enter the system of governance. Governance in service of those who are not in power necessitates additional emotive drives that exceed representation of political will. To ensure that the governance system aids collective and individual flourishing, the socio-economic context, the context of individual capability, and the lack thereof must be part of political decision-making.

Specifically, compassionate governance necessitates not only that the rational and logical system of democratic governance is well designed, but also that its constituent members, individual citizens, and the *polis* as a whole exhibit virtuous characters in service of what is morally right and just. Since flourishing is an individual and collective state of being, neither the individual nor the collective can experience *eudaimonia* without the other. And those least enfranchised (the destitute and disenfranchised) are the mirror of how well the collective is doing to attain its ends as a moral political community. Beyond representation, this requires that the overall polis have compassion for the weak and the politically "incapable." Conditions of political participation would be the ability to resonate with the suffering of others and to exhibit *agape* for the disenfranchised, rather than alignment of interests of those in power on behalf of the representation of majority interests. Critics may argue that compassionate governance is paternalistic. However, this framework does not imply that the disenfranchised are incapable of helping themselves. Rather, it acknowledges systemic inequities and aims to provide the support necessary for all individuals to achieve their full potential. By ensuring that the least enfranchised are not left behind, compassionate governance fosters a more just and equitable society.

To counterbalance the inherent amoral impetus described by Morgenthau and the moral failings Niebuhr identifies, compassionate governance integrates structural and normative methods that prioritize empathy and support for the disenfranchised. This ensures a more integrative approach to governance that promotes both individual and collective flourishing. Such an approach would follow the following logic: Those who are already in power have no inherent right to remain in power. They must derive their representational function from their ability to support the disenfranchised. In addition, those who are disenfranchised and lack the conditions for flourishing would be granted legal rights to demand what they need to attain *eudaimonia*. The difference from the current democratic welfare state, where the collective will is expressed though voting and organized protest, is that only through individual entitlements can the disenfranchised demand the fulfillment of the preconditions of *eudaimonia* within a normative framework of economic, social, and cultural rights, such as the International Covenant on Economic, Social and Cultural Rights (ICESCR). A governance of compassion would dictate that a democratic decision is not one of a representation of the will of the many but rather a commitment of the many to help those who are less able to help themselves. As such, for example, lottocratic representation would be equally suitable as long as political responsibility lies in an assessment of how well government serves the most vulnerable and not the most powerful. In such a compassionate governance structure, the principle of distributive justice in the service of compassion would be the ruling principle that moderates all other principles of governance. It would also translate into an economy of compassion that is not based on reducing costs under the dictate of efficiency for the benefit of profit, but rather on including the externalities (such as environmental and social impact) that are usually not considered as part of the cost of production. Such gains in efficiency under the condition of beneficence could contribute to reducing the difference between what those at the very bottom of the income chain presently have and what they would need to attain flourishing.

In conclusion, compassionate governance provides a necessary recalibration of democratic systems to fulfill the vision of *eudaimonia* articulated by Aristotle and address the moral deficiencies highlighted by Niebuhr. By embedding compassion and moral imperatives into the fabric of governance, we can create a system that ensures the flourishing of all members of society — a system that it not guided solely by reason but by the inherent emotive qualities of compassionate citizenry.

References

Aristotle. (2013). *Politics* [2nd ed.] (C. Lord, Trans.). Chicago University Press. http://archive.org/details/AristotlesPoliticsLord2nd.num. (Original work published ca. 350 B.C.E.)

Aristotle. (2000). *Nicomachean Ethics* (R. Crisp, Trans.). Cambridge University Press. (Original work published ca. 350 B.C.E.)

Miller, F. (2022). Supplement to Aristotle's Political Theory: Characteristics and Problems of Aristotle's Politics. *Stanford Encyclopedia of Philosophy.* https://plato.stanford.edu/Entries/aristotle-politics/supplement1.html

Morgenthau, H. J. (1945). The Evil of Politics and the Ethics of Evil. *Ethics* 56(1), 1–18.

Mulgan, R. G. (1974). Aristotle's Doctrine that Man is a Political Animal. *Hermes* 102(3), 438–45.

Niebuhr, R. (2013). *Moral Man and Immoral Society: A Study in Ethics and Politics.* Westminster John Knox Press. (Original work published 1932)

DEMOCRACY BETWEEN PLURAL KNOWLEDGE SYSTEMS

MADHULIKA BANERJEE

In the twenty-first century, we are confronted with the problem of an urgent climate crisis, for which we need to identify and decide upon the correct responses. At the heart of the crisis is a production system that is guided by a logic of rational production. This logic views nature as a "resource" to be optimized in terms of standardized mass production, to be sold at low prices yet yield great profit. Viewing nature as a resource assumes an unlimited supply available for production, which seems irrational at first. But the system of continuous new scientific knowledge creation that has generated synthetic substitutes for natural products has made it work, that is until now. The realization in the last few decades that these substitutes are not only *not* biodegradable, but also have the capacity to harm living nature in devastating ways, and that no layer of the natural environment, from the lithosphere to the atmosphere, can escape that harm, is one of the points of crisis. The other stems from the fact that the resources required to power the technologies developed from scientific knowledge are usually non-renewable fossil fuels that are being used continuously by a fundamentally consumerist society. The emissions arising from the use of these technologies are possibly the most significant causes of the climate crisis. While there is now greater investment in green technologies, the pace of this investment is not nearly as fast as it needs to be, as the earlier returns on investment in fossil fuels have yet to be fully realized; additionally, patterns of consumption are not expected to change soon.

Modern knowledges, however, have undoubtedly also built positive imaginations — of saving human labor (e.g., washing machines, harvester combines), of the good life (e.g., heating and cooling systems, the automobile), previously unimaginable machinery that has made life so exciting (airplanes and computers) — and have also introduced the ability to explore and understand nature much better (microscopes, advanced experimentation, and satellites). They have also expanded the understanding of nature and the universe, allowing everyone to understand — contrary to the oppressive authority of the church over knowledge in earlier times. Science has democratized knowledge such that it can be learned and practiced by everyone. These are radical achievements in human history, enabled and sustained by the power of the modern nation-state and big capital.

There are two problems related to the making and practice of this knowledge, however. All new knowledge created in science is to be created by "experts" who have the authority to create this new knowledge: science is for the common person, but not of and by them. This has implied a sharp distinction between theory and practice. Further, knowledge about nature has become knowledge *over* nature — about using, controlling, and replicating nature. So, in fact, these are undemocratic aspects of science but, given legitimacy by the powers that be, these aspects have become the common sense of the modern period. And it is the latest and most extreme version of this common sense that is responsible for what we call the climate crisis today. This status quo and its impact on the earth have been summarized well by Rockström et al. (2023, p. 102):

> *Humanity is well into the Anthropocene, the proposed new geological epoch where human pressures have put the Earth system on a trajectory moving rapidly away from the stable Holocene state of the past 12,000 years, which is the only state of the Earth system we have evidence of being able to support the world as we know it. These*

rapid changes to the Earth system undermine critical life-support systems, with significant societal impacts already felt, and they could lead to triggering tipping points that irreversibly destabilize the Earth system. These changes are mostly driven by social and economic systems run on unsustainable resource extraction and consumption. Contributions to Earth system change and the consequences of its impacts vary greatly among social groups and countries. Given these interdependencies between inclusive human development and a stable and resilient Earth system, an assessment of safe and just boundaries is required that accounts for Earth system resilience and human well-being in an integrated framework.

During the time that the production system described above developed in practice, a large part of humanity continued using inherited systems of production, consumption, and distribution. A range of knowledge systems — for growing food, making clothing, building homes, healing the sick, crafting tools and a range of machinery — were able to support smaller communities, efficiently and equitably, in terms of basic needs. Some of these knowledge systems also developed large production capacities such that they were able to trade in substantial quantities with markets far across the world, for example, handwoven cloth from India. Two characteristics marked these systems. The first was the belief that all human beings are part of nature and dependent on her bounty, so using the resources of nature required prudence; likewise, nature was dependent on us to regenerate, so the relationship between human beings and nature was one of interdependence. The second was that knowledge of production was carried by producers themselves, who not only inherited the learning, but also were considered capable of creating new knowledge — as innovation or in completely new frames. So, while there were hierarchies amongst practitioners, there wasn't a complete divide between the creation of knowledge and its practice. In these two respects, non-modern knowledges were deeply democratic. While they were also clearly used by human beings to further their own interests, the self-limiting character of these knowledge systems, through clear principles and restraints on usage of natural resources, respected the regenerative cycles of nature, thus not destroying it.

With the mounting hegemony of modern knowledge of production beginning about three hundred years ago, however, these systems were declared obsolescent and, because they could not match the quantities and prices of the new products, were competed out of existence. But in some places they have survived, even thrived, because people continued to believe in and rely on what they had. These people adapted their inherited knowledges to contemporary situations, making adaptations in the technical/economic aspects of production, consumption, and distribution, and mobilizing communities towards these ends, while trying to remain faithful to the world views of their knowledge systems. These world views rested on the fundamental relationship of respect for and the awareness of being an integral part of the natural world, as indicated above. This enabled human beings to use resources from nature carefully, then leave it to regenerate as a matter of principle so that it could be used again. This idea manifests itself in different ways depending upon the context. In Hindu philosophy, for example, nature, which is comprised in five forms — earth, water, fire, air, and space — is to be found in the human body. So, the individual is a microcosm of the universe. Hence, the survival of the individual depends upon and is contingent upon the survival of all natural forms, which includes other human beings in society. The circle of life is therefore complete by human beings connecting to all other living forms, making each one's survival equally important. This worldview, when manifest in production systems, makes for specific kinds of practices of production, consumption, and distribution.

The core principles of these "non-modern" knowledge systems are thus local production and consumption, though there are well-recorded systems of trade with distant places in the pre-modern period, through routes like the Silk Road. Local ecology guided production, whether of agriculture, metal work, cloth, or pottery; it influenced practices of seed saving and seed sharing, the very careful collection of medicinal plants or any forest produce such that the plant source is never destroyed; using clay from local waterbodies and not from afar for the making of utensils; using thread that comes from local cotton or mulberry trees for weaving — a range of everyday practices that reiterates the relationship of interdependence between human beings and nature. These core principles of production also made for a special virtue of the products — that of their great diversity and variety, reflecting the diversity of the natural ecological zones they came from. The emphasis on detail was primary, and the quality of a product was judged by it adhering to the principles of the overall system of production, rather than everything looking perfectly the same or homogenous. Hence products were both very diverse and of very high quality. Patterns of consumption, too, were different. By and large, things produced within a limited radius were consumed within that radius, given that each ecological zone would have its own production system according to the resources nature gave it. This is how communities living in what we describe as deserts can be so abundant and rich (Mishra, 2016).

What made these production and consumption systems possible was the significant knowledge held by these communities — of the sources of water and how to manage them to fulfil human needs; of the specific plant varieties that could grow in different soils and seasons; of different forms of pest management (with natural pesticides and through multi-cropping); of varieties of building techniques using the best local materials (mud, grass, wood, stone, lime), of adapting solar energy to construct dwellings that provided protection and comfort through all kinds of weather — there were numerous kinds of knowledge. It's possible that the technical genius and veracity of these knowledges have yet to be understood in all of their complexity. Further, how the products from these systems were distributed and the systems of circulation that made them "viable", even profitable for the producers, has been documented in some parts of the world by historians of trade, customary law, and community environmental practices. These studies need to be revisited to see to what extent these production systems survive, why they declined, and what factors can be worked on to revitalize them. It is important to make the current ecosystem amenable to allow these systems to function again so that their primary virtues of decentralization, diversity, and democratic production can be made significant again.

Whenever this argument is made, however, the response is the fear that there is an urge to turn the clock back on progress in a regressive way. It is important to remember that there is never the possibility of turning the clock back, but it is possible to affect an adaptation of these knowledge systems to our contemporary time, through their recovery and revitalization. The irony is that in many parts of the world considered "underdeveloped" these knowledge systems still survive in some measure, and this revitalization process will be easier to affect than in many societies that have marched far along the development trajectory. They can turn being neglected by modern development processes into an actual advantage here, because the revitalization process can help them move straight into a sustainable future.

The third important aspect of the practice of these knowledges was the way the communities organized the principles on which resources would be used, exchanged, shared, and even donated. Nature worship was one of the earliest practices for this reason — treating some parts of the commons as sacred meant that if they were used in any way it would represent abuse and lead to censure. Hence sacred groves, ponds, and hills were part of the discourse of commons expressly held for the common good. Across the world, these principles are recognizable in different phrases like *buen vivir*, *ubuntu*, and *swaraj* (Kothari, 2019), which treat what is available in nature as commons, to be held by everyone, with elaborate principles and systems of usage and reciprocity built into them, within the cycles of nature. These commons were also administered and negotiated locally, and also between communities that had reciprocal contributions to each other's production systems, for instance between settled farming communities and nomadic herders. Political consolidation of empires notwithstanding, these rules of custom were rarely disturbed, because those who ran kingdoms understood and accepted that the logic of managing the commons had to be a local system.

The three aspects I've described above demonstrate how knowledge held by people and communities across the world for millennia had democratic elements in its practice. These systems could accommodate differences between them because practices were guided by the logic of different kinds of nature to which the systems belonged. This also enabled exchange of knowledge and information between the communities, collaboration and cooperation, and mutual learning and sharing even across far-flung communities long before the age of modern communication. The virtues of these systems therefore make such knowledge traditions significant potential contributors to responses to the climate crisis.

At the same time, it is important to address and confront the many undemocratic aspects of these knowledges in practice. These are undemocratic practices relating to gender, caste, indigenous people, and class, depending upon the context. The very worldviews of nature and production that I have celebrated above also carried elements of deep discrimination against women and instituted hierarchies of power between and within different communities of production. These undemocratic aspects are often veiled and justified, but when these systems are examined closely and critically, this division entrenched through the binaries of gender and other ascriptive descriptions can easily be challenged. Using the modern concept of equality, which is enshrined in modern constitutions, this is a challenge that needs to be taken up politically, in all spheres of the economy: in production, consumption, and distribution. Women and other previously forbidden groups taking up work in these production systems, for example, have initiated such changes. I believe that the exciting prospect of a contemporary revitalization of these knowledge systems offers an opportunity to democratize them in these respects, while accessing and adapting the other valuable parts.

So then, how does this essay help us understand a democracy of knowledges? And what does that have to do with democracy? Faced with the climate crisis, a need to recognize the value of non-modern knowledge systems is being felt world-wide, including in the international climate reports written by scientists. But the hierarchy of knowledges in most societies — that is the undemocratic relationship that exists between modern and non-modern knowledges — prevents actualization. Therefore, a democracy of knowledges would mean two things. First, democratizing the relationship between science and other knowledges by expanding the democratic imagination to include the "pluriverse of knowledges" rather than merely the "Universe of Science." This would do away with having to choose between the two and would not represent a "turning back" from one to the other. The second would emerge from revitalizing non-modern knowledges that rest on the interdependent relationship between human beings and nature; asserting interdependence with rather than mastery over nature would democratize the relationship between human beings and nature. Just as democracy for human beings is based on human rights, this democratic imagination of rights could be expanded to equally include everything in nature, such as rivers, forests, oceans, deserts. Thus a unique and new facet of democracy would foundationally address the most urgent crisis of our time, the climate crisis.

References

Kothari, A. (2019). *Pluriverse: A Post-Development Dictionary*. Tulika Books.

Mishra, A. (2016). *Radiant Raindrops of Rajasthan* (M. Jani, Trans.). Research Foundation for Science Technology and Ecology. (Original work published 1995).

Rockström, J. et al. (2023). Safe and Just Earth System Boundaries. *Nature*, *619*, 102–111. https://doi.org/10.1038/s41586-023-06083-8

INTERSECTIONS & INTERVENTIONS: BLACK FEMINISM IN THE AGE OF THE POLYCRISIS

MINNA SALAMI

Polycrisis

Definition: (noun) a time of great disagreement, confusion, or suffering that is caused by many different problems happening at the same time so that they together have a very big effect[1]

Similar Terms: Permacrisis, Multicrisis

Usage: "In the polycrisis the shocks are disparate, but they interact so that the whole is even more overwhelming than the sum of the parts." (Adam Tooze, *Financial Times*[2])

[Alternative] *Polycrisis*

[Alternative] *Definition*: (noun) a deeply concerning and troubled period haunted by both physical and metaphysical ghosts of ontological errors and "Europatriarchal" power dynamics

[Alternative] *Similar Terms*: Metacrisis, Systemic Oppression, Europatriarchal Rule

[Alternative] *Usage*: Continue reading ...

---

1   Definition of "polycrisis" from the *Cambridge Advanced Learner's Dictionary & Thesaurus*, Cambridge University Press. Retrieved from https://dictionary.cambridge.org/dictionary/english/polycrisis.

2   Tooze, A. (2022, October 28). Welcome to the World of the Polycrisis. *Financial Times*. www.ft.com/content/498398e7-11b1-494b-9cd3-6d669dc3de33

Coined in the 1990s by the sociologist Brigitte Kern and the French philosopher Edgar Morin in their book *Homeland Earth*, the term "polycrisis" describes how multiple crises across climate, the economy, politics, health, and society are compounding and exacerbating each other. In 2022, the term resurfaced and became a buzzword. It now frames discussions at the World Bank, the World Economic Forum, and Davos, to name only a few of the high-level spaces it features in.

When a term gains such explosive traction within key institutions, it becomes important to engage with it. This is particularly important for feminists. Patriarchal power typically takes refuge in high-level decision-making and agenda-setting platforms, which is precisely where the term polycrisis also travels. The word "crisis" is itself code for issues that concern the "big boys" — decision-makers and technocrats who are usually white male elites, whereas the polycrisis most adversely impacts women, and brown and Black people as a group.

Biases in problem-solving have not put an end to global crises in the past, and they won't do so now either. In fact, they lie at the root of these crises. I provide an alternative definition of the term polycrisis to start this chapter as a sardonic play on words, but there is a truth behind it. This essay will show that the polycrisis is not only a *diagnostic* of interlocking and simultaneous threats, but also a *result* of multiple and intersecting oppressions. The polycrisis is not only a structural and economic crisis, it is also a crisis of meaning and a crisis of relationships. The unusual pairing of Black feminism and the polycrisis allows a deeper structural and affective understanding of the critical reality of our planet.

For a long time, we have been ruled by a worldview where we are masters of our destiny; where we can do as we please with our planet, and then fix the damage with technology and science. We have accepted this technoscientific way because we have constructed the world based on the idea that *all* reality is of a material nature, and that the supposedly material nature of reality is therefore measurable and quantifiable. This belief has in return produced a mindset that we can control *Nature*, a notion that I capitalize to indicate that I include in it *all* that exists: matter, land, soil, resources, humans, subatomic particles, time, and so on.

This perception creates all kinds of problems because if something needs to be material to be real, then everything which does not easily lend itself to measurement — emotions, intuition, lived experience, for example — is either neglected or forced into a rigid binary formula where it loses its telos. Inevitably, the attempt to control Nature, mysterious and untamable as it is, leads to systems that — be they economic, political, social, or educational — view Nature as a resource to endlessly exploit. Nature consists of more than tangible materiality. There are also non-material, metaphysical qualities within Nature: experience, language, subjective emotions, embodied processes, consciousness. This is also the case with democracy: we focus disproportionately on the materiality of democracy (votes, constitutions, data, etc.), all the while losing the game to those agents who understand that appealing to the immaterial elements of lived experience is a valuable strategy in recruiting people toward anti-democratic dogmas.

If we lived on another planet, we might continue believing that our sophisticated institutions can heroically end the polycrisis with their straight-out technoscientific diagnostics. But we have reached a critical juncture of increasing droughts, melting glaciers, and a natural environment undergoing rapid and threatening transformation. It is a tipping point of democratic decline, economic recession, growing social inequality, global pandemics, and immense mental and emotional suffering. There's a need for deeper and alternative approaches to crisis.

Those who are the most affected by multiple and overlapping crises need to have a say in how we address these crises. Marginalized, minoritized, and disenfranchised groups have a grasp of crisis that is not only theoretical but also experiential. This makes them less likely to formulate duplicitous "solutions" to the polycrisis. Take, for example, how Germany — world leader in recycling — exports an annual average of one million tons of plastic waste to poorer countries. Our planet's oceans and forests do not care about recycling awards. This kind of "waste colonialism" harms Germany's people as much as any other group in the long term. Any true effort to end the polycrisis must therefore understand that lurking beneath the term polycrisis are the inimical ghosts of inequality — imperialism, capitalism, racism, and patriarchy.

Wherever there is an abuse of power, there is a crisis. The debate about the polycrisis is, therefore, fundamentally a debate about power. The polycrisis forces us, yet again, to address questions of who shapes and defines reality, the direction of the planet and its human and non-human inhabitants. Every issue that informs the polycrisis, be it declining democracy, climate emergency, war, poverty, social unrest, or health threats, is enlarged by this prevailing connection of power with social hierarchy. We cannot, therefore, discuss the multiple unfolding crises without discussing the nature of hegemonic power. The biased Europatriarchal approach to the polycrisis is unsuitable for tackling the polycrisis because it is the polycrisis.

Imagine our planet at an intersection of a huge traffic jam with cars coming from multiple directions simultaneously crashing into it. Imagine that each car at this destructive intersection represents a harmful system or event, such as climate crisis, authoritarianism, surveillance capitalism, imperialism, pandemics, consumerism, militarism, hierarchism, and so on, and that our home, Earth, is being synchronically hit by each one. That *is* the image of the polycrisis.

Now replace in your mind's eye the image of the planet at the intersection of a traffic jam with an image of a Black woman at the center of the crossroads. Where the planet is at a destructive intersection of harmful systems, picture the Black woman similarly being hit by multiple vehicles representing oppressive structures, such as sexism from one lane and racism from another.

This latter image is, of course, precisely the one famously provided by the Black feminist legal scholar Kimberlé Crenshaw in 1989 when she coined the term "intersectionality". Crenshaw argued that rather than relying on single-axis feminist and Black antiracist frameworks that ignore Black women's experiences by respectively treating gender and race as exclusive categories, race and gender should be understood as inseparable factors that interdependently negate Black women's agency. To describe intersectionality, Crenshaw wrote:

> *Discrimination, like traffic through an intersection, may flow in one direction, and it may flow in another. If an accident happens in an intersection, it can be caused by cars travelling from any number*

of directions and, sometimes, from all of them. Similarly, if a Black woman is harmed because she is in the intersection, her injury could result from sex discrimination or race discrimination. (Crenshaw, 1989, p. 139)

Ultimately, Crenshaw notes, "the intersectional experience is greater than the sum of racism and sexism" (ibid., p. 140).

Intersectionality, then, describes the unique predicament of a Black woman facing multiple compounding systemic oppressions, and the polycrisis likewise describes the unique predicament of our planet being hit by multiple interlocking and systemic crises. The image of a Black woman at the intersection of an accident that blurs the lines of oppression also shows us how our planet is harmed by multiple and simultaneous systemic dangers. I have extrapolated intersectional theory to the polycrisis to demonstrate one of the reasons why Black feminist thought is necessary in the polycrisis discourse.

In the years since Crenshaw's coinage of intersectionality, Black feminist thought has expanded to also consider intersections with class, sexuality, disability, and more. Like all feminist theory, Black feminist thought has focused on the systemic nature of power structures, but Black feminist thought has been especially insightful in highlighting the ways that power is abused through multiple dimensions. Indeed, intersectionality has had a remarkable impact not only on feminist scholarship, but it has also become widely adapted and expanded geographically, topically, and methodologically to suit many possible situations, including in politics, governance, and education. The German government, for instance, created a new feminist foreign policy in 2023 in which it adopts an "intersectional approach," emphasizing the need to stand up "for everyone who is pushed to societies' margins because of their gender identity, origin, religion, age, disability or sexual orientation." Notably, prodigious scholars, such as Patricia Hill Collins and Jennifer C. Nash, have developed bodies of work that situate intersectionality in a larger theoretical and political project with "visionary world-making capacities" and, therefore, also challenge intersectionality "to broaden its reach to theorize an array of subject experiences" (Nash, 2008, p. 10).

However, Black feminists do not only have things to say about biases and structural oppression in addressing the polycrisis. As a school of thought, Black feminism also addresses the rigid and technocratic ways we address crises in the first place. It is easy for exclusionary and destructive biases to slip into the strategic frameworks because their nature is mechanical and lacking in the human touch of experience. Since the inception of Black feminist thought, the arts, the poetry, the ritual, and the embodied practice has been essential to Black feminism precisely because they confirm an understanding of reality that is about more than just the material. Due to our position outside the center of power, Black feminists have always integrally understood that we need new ontologies and ways of knowing, which don't worship quantification to the detriment of other sources of knowledge.

Specific Black feminist theories expound on this insight, such as the sociologist Patricia Hill Collins' "ethics of caring". According to Collins, the psychological effect of bearing the impacts of classism, sexism, and racism mark Black and African women's lives around the world with a unique tendency that she calls an ethics of caring. Founded upon three pillars, the ethics of caring includes, first, the value of individual expression; second, the value of emotions; and third, the capacity for empathy. Collins argues that African humanist and feminist principles influence Black women's ways of knowing. Similarly, in her body of work, the Black feminist thinker Audre Lorde built a philosophical view that encourages transformation not only through rationalizing but also through qualities such as the erotic and the poetic.

In my book *Sensuous Knowledge: A Black Feminist Approach for Everyone* (Salami, 2020), I offer a similar language with which to counter the oppressive systems that create destructive collisions at both the level of the individual and the planet. Black feminist thought helps us to reconceptualize the planet. The planet emerges as agentic, meaning it is something that acts, and that acts in relationship with other agentic entities – other planets, humans, non-humans, matter, and non-matter. These relationships are impacted by the planet and, vice versa, the planet is impacted by them. The planet illuminates the impact of metaphysics and materiality on the human and the image of the Black woman at the intersection can be extrapolated to shine a light on the destruction of the planet. Intersectionality helps us envision how symbiotic relations between agents can be transformative for both metaphysical and material outcomes.

The prefix *poly* connotes plurality, and the notion of a *crisis* is not only a situation of danger but can also signify a turning point. We can infer from these conceptual roots that, yes, the polycrisis is the doomed scenario of intersecting dangers that our world is grappling with – but the polycrisis also presents a possibility for multitudinous transformation. If it takes a state of despair to abandon biased, dualist, and un-alive ways of structuring the world, then Black feminist thought has new visions and "solutions" to heal our wounded planet.

I may be rushing ahead of myself with such a hopeful and optimistic mindset, but amidst the many fires there is also an unexpected possibility to satisfy the yearning for connections between humans and the planet, and between humans ourselves. The intention of this essay is not to provide a full articulation of these critical, imaginative, and restorative visions, but rather to sketch the contours of a powerful Black feminist intervention in the narrative of polycrisis. If the polycrisis doesn't make us tend to the wound, then what will?

References

Collins, P. H. (1990). *Black Feminist Thought: Knowledge, Consciousness, and the Politics of Empowerment*. Routledge.

Crenshaw, K. (1989). Demarginalizing the Intersection of Race and Sex: A Black Feminist Critique of Antidiscrimination Doctrine, Feminist Theory, and Antiracist Politics. *The University of Chicago Legal Forum. Feminism in the Law: Theory, Practice and Criticism*, 1989(1), 139–167. https://chicagounbound.uchicago.edu/uclf/vol1989/iss1/8/

German Federal Foreign Office. (2023). *Shaping Feminist Foreign Policy: Federal Foreign Office Guidelines*. www.shapingfeministforeignpolicy.org/papers/Guidelines_Feminist_Foreign_Policy.pdf

Nash, J. C. (2008). Re-thinking Intersectionality. *Feminist Review*, 89(1), 1–15. https://doi.org/10.1057/fr.2008.4

Salami, M. (2020). *Sensuous Knowledge: A Black Feminist Approach for Everyone*. Zed Books.

FROM CLIMATE COLONIALITY TO PLURIVERSALIZING DEMOCRACY

TOBIAS MÜLLER

Is it too late for climate justice? For the environmental justice scholar Kyle Whyte[1], the damning verdict is yes. Whyte's perspective reminds us of an inconvenient truth. As an enrolled member of the Citizen Potawatomi Nation, a federally recognized tribe located in Oklahoma, he points out a central contradiction in our attempts to address the climate crisis: interventions to achieve climate justice require healthy relationships between peoples and the land. Since these relationships have been shredded by centuries of colonialism and extractivism, any large-scale climate policy risks further aggravating existing injustices, causing further devastation, particularly to Indigenous Peoples.

If we take this problem seriously, what does this mean for our understanding of democracy and climate change? I argue that our democratic responses to climate change have been limited by ignoring the knowledges of those most affected and most fervently struggling against socio-ecological destruction. These are Indigenous and other peoples fighting for sovereignty over their lands, their cultures, and their livelihoods. It is also those who are affected by floods, food insecurities, droughts, and wars

1   Kyle Whyte is currently a member of the White House Environmental Justice Advisory Board under President Biden.

exacerbating socioecological pressures. To understand how narrow the knowledge is that informs most existing democratic systems, we need nothing short of an epistemic revolution. We need to move from a narrow epistemic "monoculture of the mind," as Vandana Shiva (2000) calls it, to a pluriversal democracy, in which diverse ways of knowing are the basis for collective decision-making.

Pluriversalizing democracy is therefore a movement, a seed, a growing epistemic mycelium that seeks to change the debate on climate change. Instead of considering climate change primarily through the lens of carbon emissions, we need to understand our current situation as one of "climate coloniality" (Sultana, 2022). This means we are not only trapped in runaway heating of the planet, but also in a way of thinking about politics that is epistemologically reductionist and prone to reproducing the very problems that led to the current intersecting crises in the first place. To address this, we need pluriversal ways of thinking, which means centering local, indigenous, and feminist knowledges. From this pluriversality a climate politics can emerge that is based on "planet repairs," where ecological considerations are shaped by repair and reparations for the harm done through colonialism, patriarchy, and capitalism. Reestablishing sovereignty and democratic ownership of peoples over their lands, knowledges, and means of production is a prerequisite for achieving planet repairs, and with that, climate justice.

Does such an approach ask for too much? If societies are unable to agree on adequate measures to mitigate climate change, how can we agree on much more far-reaching demands, such as dealing with legacies of colonialism and symmetrically integrating indigenous knowledge systems? This question points to the important problem of how to form democratic majorities for radical climate action. However, limiting climate politics to emissions reduction risks leaving intact the very socioeconomic structures at the root of the climate crisis. More importantly, a carbon-reductionist approach is prone to ignoring those most affected by the climate crisis, who are currently most actively resisting the ever-increasing expansion of fossil fuel projects and other forms of destructive extraction.

To achieve climate justice would mean to center healthy relationships with those most affected by and in direct confrontation with fossil fuel extractivism. As Whyte (2020) has argued, these healthy relationships need to entail consent, trust, accountability, and reciprocity. In the absence of such healthy relationship parameters, large-scale climate interventions will inevitably result in Black, Indigenous, and people of color experiencing further injustices. That is why the quest for climate justice is inextricably linked to the experiences of those who are already affected by environmental injustices. For example, this can take the form of environmental racism, where people racialized as non-white live in the most polluted areas, or they are driven away from the lands on which their livelihoods depend through land grabs for pipelines, mines, and plantations. Frequently these expropriations are carried out in the name of environmental protection. Interventions such as rewilding, decarbonization, and economic transition often limit peoples' access to ancestral lands, increase the financialization of nature, and are enforced through top-down decision-making. "Conservation tourism" can be part of the problem too. One case in point is the forced displacement of and disregard for the rights of the Indigenous Maasai people in the construction of high-end eco-tourism resorts in Tanzania and Kenya.

We have therefore already crossed what Whyte (2020) calls a "relational tipping point." This means that it is too late to repair the relations with and between marginalized people of various ethnic backgrounds in different parts of the world. At the same time, such repaired relationships are necessary to avoid further disenfranchisement and violence from climate interventions. This is particularly true for Indigenous Peoples and those relying on the fragile ecosystems that fossil fuel-based capitalism has been destroying over the past centuries.

What could a democratic response to this devastating diagnosis look like? In the following, I will outline why we need to recognize our current political and historical condition as one of climate coloniality. I will argue that decolonial and pluriversal knowledges are necessary preconditions for democratic climate action. Based on this diversification of knowledge, "planet repairs" and climate reparations are vital steps to confront climate coloniality. Failing to take these perspectives seriously means that climate action is prone to be part of the problem it tries to solve. Rather than a backward-looking exercise, this would be a pathway towards future-oriented democratic renewal — local, global, and planetary.

Why do we need to take climate coloniality seriously when thinking about democratic responses to multidimensional socio-ecological crises? The simple answer is that not taking an explicitly anti-colonial perspective means one is likely to perpetuate colonialism's enduring epistemic and material violence. Amnesia about colonial legacies and continuities takes different forms. Many proposals to address climate change, for example, through a "just transition" that focuses on creating "green jobs" by retraining fossil fuel workers, are largely oblivious of the histories of environmental destruction. This means that they frequently fail to grasp the political dimensions of how ecological destruction came about, and thereby fail to identify the systems that caused them. Most accounts of anthropogenic climate change focus on Europe's Industrial Revolution of the 19th century. What this perspective often neglects is to account for colonialism, the political project that produced the global economic structure, its railways, pipelines, supply chains, dispossessions of indigenous lands, and the cheap labor that fueled the Industrial Revolution. The extraction of some of the Industrial Revolution's most important — and most environmentally destructive — commodities, such as sugar, cotton, coffee, tea, tobacco, gold, rubber, and oil, was facilitated by imperial violence.

Colonialism has had many meanings and iterations throughout history. (Post)colonial regimes continue to shape former colonizer and colonized societies. For instance, the monetary policies of some former French colonies in West Africa are still largely determined in Paris. Schooling in Malawi is largely in English, meaning literacy levels in both the vernacular and the old colonial language remain low (see Cochrane, 2023). At the same time, colonialism also refers to a wide range of phenomena that structure the world today: Eurocentric epistemologies, economic exploitation, psychological alienation, ethno-nationalist categories, and the domination of human and more-than-human nature. Beginning in the 15th century, European colonialism relied on slavery and forced labor, resource extraction, industrial pollution, land grabbing, and degradation of social and ecological systems through plantation agriculture. Many ownership structures, trade relations, and legal arrangements that emerged during that time continue to shape the global economy today. These histories continue in the destructive externalities of economic production, for example toxic shipbreaking in Bangladesh and the petrochemically polluted so-called Cancer Alley that stretches through predominantly Black neighborhoods in Louisiana.

Today's economic extractivism also frequently exacerbates gender inequalities. For example, compensation for the land used for planting sugar cane and building the East African Crude Oil Pipeline (EACOP) in Uganda is often only paid to men. This discriminatory distribution of money increases the power of men in the home. As a result, substance abuse and domestic violence often increases, and many men abandon their rural families for a new life in the city. Similarly, well-meaning conservation efforts on a mission to "protect nature" have espoused colonial logics of expropriation, which result in violence against Indigenous Peoples. Many national parks in Africa were created by driving out indigenous populations to create the pristine nature sought by white hunting parties. This practice continues today in the luxury wildlife estates in Kenya's Maasai Mara and South Africa's Kruger National Park (see Mbaria and Ogada, 2016). Even organizations with millions-strong support bases such as the World Wildlife Fund (WWF) are complicit in such conservation violence. They have equipped rangers with training and weapons that have been used to beat up, sexually assault, and kill people living close to national parks. One such case of human rights violations concerns the Baka people in the Republic of the Congo, abuse that the youth activist group What the F**k World Wildlife Foundation (WTF WWF) has drawn attention to by occupying the WWF's London headquarters in 2021 (WTFWWF, n.d.).

Pushing out Indigenous Peoples from their ancestral lands in the name of protecting nature is a colonial continuity in climate politics today. Because the complicity of mainstream environmental organizations in these processes is largely unknown to the middle-class white people that make up the majority of their fee-paying members, there is little incentive to face up to the widely documented complicity of conservation efforts in violating Indigenous Peoples' rights. As a result, Indigenous Peoples are often excluded from the demos, eroding the possibility of democracy on the ground. Only by taking colonial histories and their lasting impact on human-ecological relations seriously can we grasp these logics. Without centering the self-determination of Indigenous Peoples, environmental and climate interventions are likely to further disempower those groups most affected by ecological destruction. This in turn renders collaborative stewardship of the Earth's remaining biodiversity impossible. This insight is key to understanding the underlying causes but also the possibility of democratic responses to the climate crisis.

Aptly summarizing these arguments, the geographer Farhana Sultana (2022) suggests that the entanglements of colonial, patriarchal, and capitalist dynamics in the transformation of the planet constitute our current moment as one of "climate coloniality." The plantation and the mine, infused with forced, enslaved, and exploited labor, are the forms of human-nature configuration that mark our age. They are the root causes of the current accelerating mass extinction, at a breathtaking rate of up to 150 species every day. The dominant focus on carbon emissions and the depoliticizing language of benchmarks, contributions, and assessments in UN climate negotiations obfuscate the political realities that have created the energy-, land- and pollution-intensive modes of production and consumption at the heart of the crisis.

What is frequently missing in policymaking at local, national, and global levels is both the experiences and the agency of the billions of people who live through the devastating effects of extractivism. Their perspectives are vital to understanding how, across the Global South, resource wealth from their territories is funneled towards multinational corporations. This process is often supported by post-colonial elites who have simply taken over as the enablers and beneficiaries of the exploitation of minerals, agricultural products, and people's cheap labor during colonialism. Confronting climate coloniality means taking seriously how power — colonial and otherwise — shapes the way we tell our human-ecological history. This is important for a democratic response to the climate crisis since many proposals for planetary and global interventions, from carbon-offsetting to geo-engineering, risk perpetuating colonial logics of decision-making. They often fail to consider those most affected and whose territories are being intervened in, let alone establish their consent and participation. This means that any attempt at "planetary democracy" is prone to perpetuate colonial logics if it is not based on a reckoning with (post)colonial histories.

If we have passed the relational tipping point, the question of whether "we" will make it "on time," reveals itself to be a highly exclusive one. Many people whose social and ecological histories have been shaped by colonialism and its enduring economic patterns are not "at risk" of experiencing some future ecological and societal collapse, as many in the Global North fear. Instead, they have been living in and resisting socio-ecological destruction for centuries. What these people have faced due to ecological colonialism — land expropriation, mass pollution, biodiversity loss, water shortages, desertification, droughts, famines, species extinction — is similar to what many peoples around the world are already experiencing, and will increasingly face, due to climate change.

This realization urges us to rethink basic assumptions about democracy. We need to build upon theory from the South, taking the real experiences of ecological devastation as the starting point for our democratic thinking, rather than treating it merely as a "policy issue" or as a distant threat. Confronting climate coloniality means bringing people from the margins into the centers of political decision-making. It requires that we interrogate the way certain peoples, and the ecosystems their survival depends on, have been structurally excluded from the possibilities of democratic futures. Pluriversalizing the knowledge systems democracies rely on is essential to meet this epochal challenge.

Pluriversalizing Democracy

How can we gain a deeper understanding of what our condition of climate coloniality means for the (im)possibilities of democratic futures? Historically, democracy has gained power to transform societies at moments when the definition of the demos was expanded. This was true when suffrage was extended to those without property, to women, and to those discriminated against based on racialized and anti-Black categorizations.

For democracies stuck in systems defined by polarization and elite capture, we can learn from this history that we need to radically extend suffrage and representation to confront the climate crisis. This should include enfranchising (climate) refugees and teenagers, who have the highest stakes in today's ecological decision-making. It should also involve extending legal standing, rights, and representation to non-human entities, such as rivers, forests, glaciers, and ecosystems. This has been attempted by the Bolivian Law of the Rights of Mother Earth, which has been championed by grassroots peasant-indigenous organizations. The original ecocentric proposal stipulated that whenever there was a conflict of interest, the protection of Mother Earth should prevail. Unfortunately, the Bolivian government only adopted a watered-down and largely ineffective version of the law and the Mother Earth Ombudsman it promised to create twelve years ago still does not exist (see Muños, 2023). Climate movements are demanding the institution of local, national, and global Climate Citizens' Assemblies with real decision-making powers. Hundreds of climate assemblies have already been run at municipal, national, and civil society levels, which demonstrates the enormous appetite for such democratic experiments.

While these are all important initiatives, they are not in themselves sufficient to deal with the root causes of climate coloniality. They leave intact the institutional pillars of capitalist nation-states, including, importantly, their ontological and epistemological underpinnings. As long as demands to "protect nature" or to "rewild" the planet exclude the most marginalized, such as those living in legal grey zones, in fragile ecosystems, and on land that does not "belong" to them according to the logic of private property, these well-intentioned calls to action simply perpetuate the same colonialist patterns. The cognitive and normative thinking that has produced structures that have pushed humankind and other species to a precipice, and many humans and species beyond it, cannot provide adequate tools with which to dismantle these same structures. Black feminist philosopher Audre Lorde's famous claim that "the master's tools will never dismantle the master's house" challenges us to think about which tools — epistemic and political — are suitable to confront climate coloniality, and which ones are prone to reproduce its logics. Colonial logics are often infused by a universalist supremacy, i.e., that one language, political system, religion, or economic form should dominate. Therefore, we need what anthropologist Arturo Escobar (2020) calls a "pluriversal politics" — meaning that frequently excluded experiences, worldviews, and knowledges should take center state. In a world of "Europatriarchal" (Salami, 2020) racial capitalism, this then would be the knowledge of women, Indigenous Peoples, grassroots movements, and spiritual traditions, especially on questions of (re)production, care, conviviality, and multi-species justice.

A democratic and decolonizing response to climate coloniality requires radical imagination and politics that center both the histories of loss, expropriation, and violence, and the practices of resistance, resilience, and transnational collaborations. This means unsettling the universalist moral and sociological assumptions that underly dominant climate discourses. Among the most salient reductionist dualisms these discourses engender are that of nature/culture, thinking/feeling, modern/traditional. Take, for example, the five strands of the "Great Leap" proposed by the 2022 Club of Rome Report *Earth for All: A Survival Guide for Humanity*: poverty, inequality, gender, food, and energy. While acknowledging some of its merits, environmentalist Ashish Kothari argues that the report is "curiously silent on the deep cultural and spiritual revolutions required and the pluriverse of cosmologies available for this" (Club of Rome, 2022). This points to the required epistemic transformations towards pluriversality that we need to decolonize climate coloniality.

From this perspective it becomes clear that beneath the alleged novelty of green politics lie epistemological and ontological continuities that must be uprooted to achieve a truly democratic and liberatory response to the climate crisis. As Sultana (2022, p. 7) succinctly puts it: "Liberation comes from destroying colonialism's impact on lands, bodies, and psyches to overcome the apocalypse that continues to be coloniality — i.e., moving from alienation and dehumanization to self-realization in order to decolonize colonial traumas." This means that a politics of liberation needs to be epistemological and discursive as well as material, embodied, and political. At the same time, these terms, like the language we use to express them, are limited tools which need to be complemented by sensemaking from other ways of worldmaking.

For example, the campaign "Stop the Maangamizi: We Charge Ecocide/Genocide" uses the Swahili word *Maangamizi* to draw attention to the interlocking effects of colonial nation building, environmental destruction, and racialized violence (Stop the Maangamizi, n.d.). Similarly, the genocide of the Herero and Nama by the Germans in Namibia or that of the Kikuyu by the British in Kenya were intimately tied to the destruction of ecosystems through plantation agriculture, mining, and pollution. These logics and effects still haunt the politics and everyday lives of postcolonial states across the continent of Africa today. Pluriversalizing democracy means democratizing the knowledges at the basis of collective decision-making and centering "herstories" and "ourstories" — the frequently neglected histories of women and grassroots communities, those who have been most affected by the double movement of ecological and political domination. This epistemic pluriversalization is a necessary requirement for a democratic politics of planetary repair.

Repairing Planet and Politics

One of the most visceral manifestations of today's intersecting crises are the proliferating colonial-ecological wounds. From deadly air pollution and toxic uranium mines, to leaking pipelines and the epidemic of sexual violence that often accompanies resource extraction, our present condition requires responses beyond the climate politics produced by the Europatriarchal (Salami, 2020), i.e., Eurocentric and patriarchal, epistemological and economic status quo. What is needed is a feminist repair of relationships. We need to repair relationships to our traumatized bodies, to our close and distant kin, the human and more-than-human, to the land, and to the collective ourstories of resistance against all that has propelled us into the age of extinction.

The fight for reparations for enslavement and colonialism has been an ongoing struggle for centuries. However, the climate crisis reveals why combining reparations and climate action might be a political project that provides a rallying point across the fractures of progressive politics. In his recent book *Reconsidering Reparations*, Olúfẹ́mi Táíwò (2022) argues that climate reparations are necessary not only to prevent backsliding of gains made by people of color in the US since the Civil Rights Movement, but they are also conducive to revitalizing communities, to improving welfare provisions, and to establishing democratic bodies where spending decisions can reestablish local agency for a just ecological transition.

The epochal significance of both the past injustices of colonialism and the future injustices of climate change means that combining the two perspectives opens up a political vision at a scale that might be able to meet the magnitude of the climate crisis. This is because planet repairs advocated for by leading reparationists, such as Esther Stanford-Xosei and Kofi Mawuli Klu, require us to fundamentally reshape the cognitive, economic, spiritual, and ecological relations of our world. While not all share this broad view, ideas in the field of climate reparations are gaining increasing traction: planet repairs, ecocide trials, climate debt cancellation, abolition ecology, the Land Back campaign to reestablish indigenous sovereignty, and a truth and reconciliation commission for the destruction of the climate are just some examples. They are all instances of the growing momentum of locally grounded and planetarily oriented efforts for ecological decolonization (see Müller and Cochrane, 2024). They are efforts "to heal colonial wounds everywhere" (Sultana, 2022, p. 7), which require new forms of democratic reckoning with the injustices of the past and the present.

Grassroots movements (very broadly understood) are crucial to bringing topics such as those discussed in this essay to public attention, as well as to shifting the "Overton window", i.e., the space of what is politically thinkable and possible. As Deva Woodly's (2021) account of the Movement for Black Lives demonstrates, grassroots movements are not merely conducive to democratic renewal, they are a democratic necessity. Movements are the loci of production of political philosophies and theories grounded in struggle, constantly pushed to evolve by those excluded by society. In these frictions, new forms of political thinking and action emerge. While they are not immune from reproducing the very pathologies they seek to overcome, self-reflective movements harbor the potential to transform the meaning of the very terms of democratic politics, such as sovereignty, representation, and freedom. Centering experiences of resistance is also necessary for healing relationships with peoples shaped by histories of imperial violence, in colonizing and colonized societies alike.

Healing and repair of planet and politics requires a multi-scalar and multi-sensual approach such as that embodied in the tricontinental vision of *ubuntupachavidya* advocated by Extinction Rebellion's Internationalist Solidarity Network (XRISN, n.d.). This approach combines the shared humanity of the Southern African concept of *ubuntu*, the Mother Earth orientation of the Abya Yalan (Latin American) concept of *pachamama*, and the comprehensive knowledge encapsulated in the South Asian concept of *vidya*. Taking the time to really understand such traditions of knowing and doing is in itself an exercise of epistemological resistance and creativity that can reshape the terms by which we understand our shifting position in the web of life.

Unlearning the ways we have looked at the world thus far and re-learning to connect to such traditions of knowledge is certainly a challenge for many and requires long-term commitment, possibly for life. This commitment to unlearn and relearn is the opposite of the allegedly quick technofixes of carbon pricing, carbon capture, and geoengineering, which leave our cognitive, economic, and political structures untouched. As with any diverse constituency, different local and indigenous communities will disagree over what concepts and cosmologies are most useful to break the deadly cycles of climate coloniality. However, making space for and listening deeply to these debates is not an insurmountable problem but rather part of the necessary process of democratic renewal.

Rallying around the pioneering work of movements for planetary, relational, and reparatory justice could bolster new approaches that shatter the destructive stranglehold of Europatriarchal universalism and extractive fossil capitalism on democratic politics. This is a prerequisite for a truly just transition that experiments with new modes of political and (more-than-)human relationships. Confronting climate coloniality is a promising pathway to think and practice how to do that, and is essential to the future of democracy.

References

Club of Rome. (2022). Endorsements for *Earth for All: A Survival Guide for Humanity*. www.clubofrome.org/wp-content/uploads/2022/08/Earth4All_Book_Endorsements.pdf

Cochrane, T. (2023). The Power of Stories: Oral Storytelling, Schooling and onto-Epistemologies in Rural Malawi. *Oxford Review of Education*, 49(4), 478–95. https://doi.org/10.1080/03054985.2023.2218609

Escobar, A. (2020). *Pluriversal Politics: The Real and the Possible*. Duke University Press. https://doi.org/10.2307/j.ctv11315v0

Mbaria, J. (2016). *The Big Conservation Lie: The Untold Story of Wildlife Conservation in Kenya*. Lens & Pens Publishing.

Müller, T., & Cochrane, T. (2024). Planetary health as Co-Liberation: Trauma, spirituality, and embodied decolonization in the climate movement. In J. Cochrane, G. Gunderson, T. Cutts, & E. Elgar (Eds.), *Handbook of Religion and Health*. http://dx.doi.org/10.2139/ssrn.4689650

Muños, L. (2023, February 6). Bolivia's Mother Earth Laws. Is the Ecocentric Legislation Misleading?. ReVista. https://revista.drclas.harvard.edu/bolivias-mother-earth-laws-is-the-ecocentric-legislation-misleading/

Salami, M. (2020). *Sensuous Knowledge: A Black Feminist Approach for Everyone*. Zed Books.

Shiva, V. (2000). *Monocultures of the Mind: Perspectives on Biodiversity and Biotechnology*. Zed Books.

Stop the Maangamizi, n.d., Stop the harm as the first step to repairing the damage. International Social Movement for Afrikan Reparations (ISMAR). https://stopthemaangamizi.com/

Sultana, F. (2022). The Unbearable Heaviness of Climate Coloniality. *Political Geography*, 99, https://doi.org/10.1016/j.polgeo.2022.102638

Táíwò, O. O. (2022). *Reconsidering Reparations: Worldmaking in the Case of Climate Crisis*. Oxford University Press.

Ubuntu Pacha Vidya. (2018.) XR Internationalist Solidarity Network. https://www.xrisn.earth/ubuntupachavidya

Whyte, K. (2020). Too Late for Indigenous Climate Justice: Ecological and Relational Tipping Points. *WIREs Climate Change*, 11(1). https://doi.org/10.1002/wcc.603

Woodly, D. R. (2022). *Reckoning: Black Lives Matter and the Democratic Necessity of Social Movements*. Oxford University Press.

WTFWWF (n.d.) Evidence of WWF abuses. https://www.wtfwwf.org/

SUSTAINABLE DEVELOPMENT CANNOT BE THE FUTURE WE WANT

LOUIS J. KOTZÉ

I. Fuck Sustainable Development!

In a 2016 article, Professor of Human Geography Simon Springer famously wrote:

> *Fuck Neoliberalism. That's my blunt message ... I have nothing positive to add to the discussion about neoliberalism, and to be perfectly honest, I'm quite sick of having to think about it. I've simply had enough ... I've been writing on the subject for many years and I came to a point where I just didn't want to commit any more energy to this endeavor for fear that continuing to work around this idea was functioning to perpetuate its hold. On further reflection I also recognize that it is potentially quite dangerous to simply stick our heads in the sand and collectively ignore a phenomenon that has had such devastating and debilitating effects on our shared world. There is an ongoing power to neoliberalism that is difficult to deny and I'm not convinced that a strategy of ignorance is actually the right approach. So my exact thoughts were, 'well fuck it then'. Why should we be more worried about using profanity than we are about the actual vile discourse of neoliberalism itself?* (Springer, 2016, pp. 285–86).

Springer's coarse sentiments resonate with me because I feel the same about the concept of sustainable development, itself a neoliberal invention that has been the focus of my work and critique for at least a decade. I intensely dislike the idea of sustainable development with the same vigor that Springer dislikes the broader neoliberal context within which palliatives such as sustainable development have been created and continue to operate.

Capitalizing on the momentum created by the 1987 Brundtland Report[1], which formally introduced the concept, sustainable development has now become the compass alongside which the world orientates its neoliberal, capitalist-centered, development vision, from the global all the way down to the local. Sustainable development has become embedded as a guiding principle for decision-making (political, economic, and otherwise) in virtually all social institutions, including, among many others, international law and the development policies of international institutions, such as the International Monetary Fund and the World Bank (Redclift, 2006).

The Sustainable Development Goals (SDGs) embody the latest near-universal agreement setting out a vision of "The Future We Want," and politically institutionalize and structurally embed sustainable development as the world's preferred grand development vision until at least 2030. The SDGs were adopted by the United Nations in 2015 (more formally known as the 2030 Agenda for Sustainable Development) and contain 17 goals and 169 targets that offer a blueprint for guiding humanity's future development course. The 2030 Agenda is based on and has been shaped by the 2012 Outcome Document of the Rio+20 Conference on Sustainable Development, titled *The Future We Want*. This document is explicit about what it considers to be its foundational norm: sustainable development. Sustainable development is therefore *the core principle* informing the

[1] The Brundtland Report, also known as "Our Common Future", was published by the United Nations and attempted to merge development and environment into a unified goal. The term "sustainable development" was created and defined as "development that meets the needs of the present without compromising the ability of future generations to meet their own needs" (p. 16).

shape of *The Future We Want*. Assuming that *The Future We Want* is, at least in part, also a democratic choice and should involve a democratic process leading us to decide what future it is that we want (i.e., who are "we," how do "we" reach consensus, do "we" also decide for non-humans, and do "we" decide for future living beings?). This is highly problematic.

From the perspective of an environmental lawyer, I am critical of sustainable development because it promises what it cannot deliver because of the oxymoron at its core, namely that infinite social-economic development is actually possible on a finite planet. Moreover, like associated concepts of "green economy" and "green growth," sustainable development has become a term, and increasingly an unquestioned mindset, that capitalist societies use to treat some of the symptoms of the problem of social-ecological decline in a light-handed way instead of addressing the core causes of this problem, namely neoliberal-driven, growth-without-limits development, over-consumption and extractivism, and exploitation and domination of vulnerable beings.

I situate my concerns and associated critique of sustainable development in the epistemic context of the Anthropocene (Steffen et al., 2015), the proposed new geological epoch that is characterized by human-induced loss of planetary resilience, loss of critical Earth system regulatory functions, fast-approaching planetary boundaries, an ever-diminishing safe operating space for humanity, unprecedented levels of rising injustice, social upheaval, and oppressive exploitation, and an increasingly uneven world order. As we gradually make our way into and through the Anthropocene (precarious as such an unpredictable journey is), given sustainable development's complicity in causing and exacerbating the drivers of the Anthropocene and its inability to address the root causes of these drivers, I believe it cannot continue to function as the foundation for future development. Reflecting on democracy and our collective role in shaping our future, sustainable development certainly cannot be a roadmap toward achieving a just world within planetary limits.

II. The Anthropocene

Although having been formally rejected by the International Commission on Stratigraphy[2], the term "Anthropocene" (loosely translated as the "age of the human") informally denotes the most recent period in Earth's geological history, which is characterized by the formidable telluric force that humans increasingly exert on planet Earth. Through scientific and technological development and progress, humans have acquired the ability to impact key Earth system regulatory functions in ways that equal earthly powers, such as volcanoes and earthquakes, instigating a Sixth Mass Extinction event (Barnosky et al., 2011).

The Anthropocene has become a widely used term-of-art in popular culture and academic debates. Although subject to critique, especially because it tends to generalize human impacts on the Earth system in an undifferentiated way that ignores global inequalities, injustices, and past and present contributions to social-ecological decay, the Anthropocene, as an episteme, offers a useful discursive space to critically re-examine our social institutions, such as law, politics, economics, and religion, which all somehow shape our relationships with each other, with other non-humans, and with non-living entities:

> [...] the Anthropocene fundamentally challenges basic assumptions of modern thought, such as: dualisms separating humans from nature, conceptions of unique human agency and the presumption of progressive norms, such as liberty, [and] that the planet is capacious enough for individual acts to be thought of as disconnected from the peoples, species and processes once rendered as 'others.' (Schmidt, Brown, and Orr, 2016, p. 188)

[2] On March 21, 2024 the International Commission on Stratigraphy and the International Union of Geological Sciences released a joint statement rejecting the proposal to adopt the Anthropocene as a formal unit of geologic time. The statement does, however, conclude that the term "[...] will remain an invaluable descriptor of human impact on the Earth system." https://stratigraphy.org/news/152

The imagery of the Anthropocene prompts us to reconceive our social institutions in ways that could possibly address, more effectively, the many challenges resulting from human encroachment on planetary limits at an Earth system scale (Gellers, 2021); elsewhere expressed as planetary boundaries (Rockström et al., 2024; Rockström et al., 2009). Our newly discovered geological human agency also means that "Anthropocene thought acquires an ethical dimension — what global society *chooses to do* impacts the planetary environmental and ecological systems that must sustain later generations" (Kennel, 2021, p. 90).³ The fact that we have a choice, and the realization that our current decisions and behavior affect not only present human and non-human generations but also future generations, will essentially require us to carefully consider what future it is that we actually want. The decisions we make now, and how we realize the objectives of these decisions and carry them through our social institutions, will fundamentally affect the interests and well-being of the living order, now and in the future.

III. The Future We Want?

The world has already decided which future it wants, at least until 2030. At the Rio+20 Conference on Sustainable Development in 2012, the United Nations General Assembly endorsed the Outcome Document *The Future We Want*. States unequivocally renewed their "commitment to sustainable development and to ensuring the promotion of an economically, socially and environmentally sustainable future for our planet and for present and future generations" (para 1) ; while they acknowledge "the need to further mainstream sustainable development at all levels, integrating economic, social and environmental aspects and recognizing their interlinkages, so as to achieve sustainable development in all its dimensions" (para 3). The Outcome Document further dedicates an entire section to laying out preparatory plans for the eventual development of the SDGs, recognizing "the importance and utility of a set of

---

3   Emphasis in the original.

sustainable development goals" that "should address and incorporate in a balanced way all three dimensions of sustainable development and their interlinkages" (para 246).

And thus, the SDGs were launched with great fanfare in 2015, copying much of the language that was used in the Rio+20 Outcome Document and reaffirming sustainable development as the rhetorical, contextual, ethical, normative, and political fulcrum on which the world's development vision revolves. One can hardly fault the lofty (and possibly sincere) undertakings by states and private sector actors to address many of the world's most critical concerns in the next few years. Who can disagree with an ambitious global resolution that aims "between now and 2030, to end poverty and hunger everywhere; to combat inequalities within and among countries; to build peaceful, just and inclusive societies; to protect human rights and promote gender equality and the empowerment of women and girls; and to ensure the lasting protection of the planet and its natural resources" (para 3)? It is encouraging, but rare, to find such high ambition in global political declarations, and when one does, it is either included in non-binding preambular provisions of a binding instrument,[4] or in the main text of non-binding instruments, such as the SDGs. States inevitably dislike binding themselves to ambitious goals, and where consensus is reached about some contentious issue, such consensus usually reflects the lowest possible common denominator that keeps everyone satisfied and in the game, as it were. The result therefore is that *The Future We Want* is fashioned around 17 ambitious, non-binding goals, while sustainable development is the foundation for achieving these goals, and therefore now constitutes the core of the world's present and future development vision.

My central thesis is that although these goals are all appropriate and desirable, they will likely never be achieved, or not achieved to their fullest possible extent, precisely because they are deeply entrenched in

---

[4] For example, one of the few provisions in international environmental law that recognizes the need for planetary "integrity," the Paris Climate Agreement, says in a preambular provision that states note "the importance of ensuring the integrity of all ecosystems, including oceans, and the protection of biodiversity, recognized by some cultures as Mother Earth, and noting the importance for some of the concept of 'climate justice,' when taking action to address climate change."

sustainable development dogma. The problem with the SDGs is therefore *sustainable development*, which is an unsound foundation on which to build and pursue a "comprehensive, far-reaching and people-centered set of universal and transformative Goals and targets" (para 2). My reason for saying so derives from a deeper critique of sustainable development dogma that I, and others, have developed over the years (e.g., Kotzé and Adelman, 2022). Here is a brief summary of the core argument:

Sustainable development, as a concept, principle, and/or goal offers nothing new, and in its SDG guise is simply old wine in a somewhat new bottle. Ever since its formal inception in the 1987 Brundtland Report, sustainable development has not been an ambitious undertaking: we simply need to somehow balance social, economic, and environmental concerns and celebrate those (rare) instances where the three circles converge (and to this day they have never converged fully in any meaningful way). The bar was set very low by the Brundtland Report, which was a disingenuous compromise suppressing the contradiction between the ideal of endless extractive growth on the one hand and real and sobering planetary limits on the other hand. Possibly, also with the hope of under-promising and over-delivering (although the latter has rarely happened in the course of history), more ambitious legal and political goals, such as ecological sustainability or planetary integrity, have consistently been rejected by states precisely because they significantly raise the level of normative ambitious and political commitment and the extent and depth of action to be taken by states on specific matters (Bosselmann, 2016).

Sustainable development very conveniently provided that perfect balance between catchy rhetoric and lofty ideals that can appease all stakeholders, while imposing minimal obligations on states to take drastic actions to, for example, reign in carbon intensive industries, or provide free universal healthcare and public transport for everyone. After all, the Brundtland Commission's impossible brief was to square the circle of growth as a precondition for development and environmental protection. The Brundtland definition of sustainable development possessed a conceptual ambiguity that made it palatable to the widest possible audience. It was broad enough to capture the energy of this environmental reawakening and to resonate with the increasingly international nature of popular thinking about environmental problems.

Its central concern for equity with present and future generations retained sufficient idealism to garnish the support of ecological purists and advocates for distributive justice. Yet its vague, contradictory stance on ecological limits and economic processes weakened that very threat, leaving just enough wiggle room so that pro-growth economists, business leaders, and governments could also comfortably embrace the concept (Carruthers, 2011, p. 99).

While some will point to a few successes of sustainable development over the years (for example that it has at least managed to foster some consensus among nations about the dire state of the world), it has not managed to actually set the world on a more *sustainable* developmental path. The world is probably worse off than in 1987, which is why we needed to create a comprehensive, multi-faceted set of SDGs to get us out of the impossibly tight spot we find ourselves in. But in doing so, we are using the same medicine to treat an illness that it could never cure, while the illness has become infinitely more severe. To be sure, the conclusion of a recent mid-term assessment of the literature investigating the political steering effects of the SDGs is that, on balance, the SDGs are not fully geared toward steering, nor actually capable of facilitating, the sort of transformations we urgently need (Biermann, Hickmann, and Sénit, 2022).

The reality is that the Anthropocene's planetary crisis is so urgent and profound that any future development vision requires a fundamentally different worldview — one that offers a genuinely ambitious and appropriate solution for the problem that it aims to solve. The stark disconnect between the low ambition of sustainable development and the gravity of the planetary crisis that we observe through the lens of the Anthropocene suggests that sustainable development, to the extent that it manifests in the SDGs as the roadmap for future development, will simply reinforce the status quo ante. As the world continues to recommit itself to sustainable development over and over again, despite convincing evidence that this dogma cannot bring about the radical transformations we urgently need in the Anthropocene, *The Future We Want* inevitably remains the past we have inherited and the present we now experience. Nothing has changed and nothing will unless we discard sustainable development and urgently search for a new ethic that sees development not only in terms of material gain, but also as a way to care for a planet in crisis and the vulnerable present and future living order it hosts.

While there are other ethics, such as those rooted in Indigenous cosmovisions and the "rights of nature" theory, the recently proposed notion of the "planetary commons" offers a potent alternative foundation to start tracing the outlines of what a different democratic future in the Anthropocene might look like (Rockström et al., 2024). The idea of the planetary commons is based on, but significantly expands, the traditional notion of the global commons. The planetary commons include critical biophysical Earth-regulating systems and their functions, irrespective of where they are located, because they are essential to sustaining all life across the planet, including the stability of our societies. The planetary commons framework is informed by Anthropocene dynamics and includes, as its core rationale, the need to safeguard and steward critical Earth system functions that regulate the stability of the planet and sustain its resilience, avoid breaching planetary boundaries that cause tipping point risks, and work toward ensuring a just and inclusive world for everyone, now and in the future (Rockström et al., 2024). As we enter the Deep Anthropocene, the idea of the planetary commons offers an epistemic framework to creatively develop alternative, more radical, innovative, and contextualized forms of planetary care, while it explicitly rejects predatory paradigms such as sustainable development. More specifically, "commoning" shows us how it might be possible to co-create governance regimes for Earth's destabilized critical regulatory processes and functions that are not yet governed or are governed inadequately. "Commoning" also implies shared governance that offers pathways for democratic representation of present and future human and non-human generations. It simultaneously offers the possibility to craft planetary stewardship obligations that both states and a wide range of non-state actors, such as corporations and civil movements, should embrace. A new global governance constellation that starts with the idea that better protection of the planetary commons is a non-negotiable necessity as we move deeper into the Anthropocene could potentially lead to the development of democratically negotiated, shared, and ambitious goals that planetary commons governance must strive toward, such as planetary justice and planetary integrity. As we argue in detail in Rockström et al. (2024), working toward such ambitious common goals and devising ways of keeping everyone accountable to reach them, could go a long way toward optimizing the current lackluster global environmental governance regime.

References

Barnosky, A. et al. (2011). Has the Earth's Sixth Mass Extinction Already Arrived?. *Nature*, 471, 51–57. https://doi.org/10.1038/nature09678

Biermann, F., Hickmann, T., & Sénit, C-A. (Eds.). (2022). *The Political Impact of the Sustainable Development Goals: Transforming Governance Through Global Goals?* Cambridge University Press. https://doi.org/10.1017/9781009082945

Bosselmann, K. (2016). *The Principle of Sustainability: Transforming Law and Governance* (2nd ed.). Routledge. https://doi.org/10.4324/9781315553955

Carruthers, D. (2001). From Opposition to Orthodoxy: The Remaking of Sustainable Development. *Journal of Third World Studies*, 18(2), 93–112. https://www.jstor.org/stable/45193956

Gellers, J. (2021). Earth system law and the Legal Status of Nonhumans in the Anthropocene. *Earth System Governance*, 7, 1–8. https://doi.org/10.1016/j.esg.2021.100126

Higgs, K. (2014). *Collision Course: Endless Growth on a Finite Planet.* MIT Press. https://doi.org/10.7551/mitpress/9880.001.0001

Kennel, C. F. (2020). The Gathering Anthropocene Crisis. *The Anthropocene Review*, 8(1), 83–95. https://doi.org/10.1177/2053019620957355

Kotzé L. J., & Adelman, S. (2022). Environmental Law and the Unsustainability of Sustainable Development: A Tale of Disenchantment and of Hope. *Law and Critique*, 1–22. https://doi.org/10.1007/s10978-022-09323-4

Lafferty, W. (1996). The Politics of Sustainable Development: Global Norms for National Implementation. *Environmental Politics*, 5(5), 185–208. https://doi.org/10.1080/09644019608414261

Redclift, M. (2006). Sustainable Development (1987–2005): An Oxymoron Comes of Age. *Horizontes Antropológicosm*, 12(25), 65–84. https://doi.org/10.1590/S0104-71832006000100004

Rockström, J. et al. (2024). The planetary commons: A new paradigm for safeguarding Earth-regulating systems in the Anthropocene. *Proceedings of the National Academy of Sciences*, 121(5). https://doi.org/10.1073/pnas.2301531121

Rockström, J. et al. (2009). A Safe Operating Space for Humanity. *Nature*, 461, 472–475. https://doi.org/10.1038/461472a

Schmidt, J., Brown, P., & Orr, C. (2016). Ethics in the Anthropocene: A Research Agenda. *The Anthropocene Review*, 3(3), 188–200. https://doi.org/10.1177/2053019616662052

Springer, S. (2016). Fuck Neoliberalism. ACME: *An International Journal for Critical Geographies*, 15(2), 285–292. https://doi.org/10.14288/acme.v15i2.1342

Steffen, W. et al. (2015). The Trajectory of the Anthropocene: The Great Acceleration. *The Anthropocene Review*, 2(1), 81–98. https://doi.org/10.1177/2053019614564785

United Nations. (2012). *The Future We Want: Outcome Document of the Rio+20 Conference on Sustainable Development.* https://sustainabledevelopment.un.org/futurewewant.html

II

SEEDS
FOR REPAIR

TACKLING DISCOURSIVE POLARIZATION: WELCOME RADICAL IDEAS BUT NOT AGGRESSION!

MICHAEL BRÜGGEMANN

"Since wars begin in the minds of men, it is in the minds of men that the defences of peace must be constructed." This is the first sentence of the Constitution of the United Nations Educational, Scientific and Cultural Organization (UNESCO). In the following paragraphs of its constitution, UNESCO identifies communication as key to creating mutual understanding between peoples and avoiding another global war (UNESCO, 2023). Yet communication and exchange may also militarize the minds of people. Political elites drive this process, instrumentalizing the emotions of people for political gain — and this will continue to be part of the political process. This essay will focus on two other actors currently shaping public opinion: professional journalism and social media networks. Both play their part in fueling discursive polarization. Most notably, they create an image of a society characterized by numerous conflicts between extreme groups that seem unwilling and unworthy of engaging in a constructive dialogue. This distorted depiction of society functions as a self-fulfilling prophesy — and this "false polarization" (Fernbach and Van Boven, 2022) polarizes debates and ultimately polarizes society.

As an example from current debates in German news media, I will focus on the issue of climate protests. News media coverage of recent protests by the group Letzte Generation (Last Generation) has paid considerable attention to disruptive protests involving young people who throw soup at paintings or glue themselves to roads, but this coverage has largely ignored their cause (climate justice). Instead, the protests have been discussed using criminal or extremist framing (for a much deeper analysis, see Meyer et al., 2023), debating, for example, whether this group is an extremist or criminal organization. This framing is driven both by conservative politicians and right-wing media outlets who had already used these frames when discussing the more conventional protests by the Fridays for Future movement. The same frames, with even more extreme claims (i.e., Last Generation members are murderers, they should go to prison), circulated widely on digital media networks. News coverage has included claims by journalists that the climate movement has polarized society — with the only evidence for this being some angry car drivers trying to push or pull the protesters from the streets. The protesters themselves have remained non-violent and their political demands have been modest: speed limits, cheaper tickets for public transport, etc.

Both professional journalism and digital platform providers could do much more in order to avoid the harmful dynamics of polarization by (1) refocusing the public's attention on the bridges that connect a pluralistic society (such as the broad support for climate protection in society), and by (2) featuring bridge-builders more prominently than destroyers of bridges (e.g., moderate critics of the protesters who nonetheless support the general legitimacy of protest). This would entail (3) *not* rewarding aggressive statements directed at the respective outgroup with media attention and (4) welcoming radical ideas, in the original sense of the word, i.e., ideas that relate to the roots of a problem. Ultimately, this may not only help to contain destructive dynamics of unconstrained polarization but would also make for better journalism and a more rewarding experience for media users. Both outcomes may actually be strong arguments for media managers and journalists to rethink current professional practices.

In the following, I will focus specifically on polarization as a challenge to liberal democracies and much of the reasoning will not apply to authoritarian regimes, where freedom of the press and rule of law are not (fully) granted. I will first explain the discursive dimension of polarization, why it may be harmful to democracy, and what kind of depolarization we should strive for. I will then argue that the logics of journalism and social media networks need to evolve in order to limit polarization. Finally, I will elaborate my suggestions on how the media could do better.

What Is Discursive Polarization and Is It Harmful?

I argue that polarization is a meta-process of social divergence: it is the process behind different indicators, which, only when taken together, are sufficient for the diagnosis of "polarization" (Brüggemann and Meyer, 2023). The two main dimensions of polarization are the ideological and the affective dimensions (e.g., as summarized in Kubin and Sikorski, 2021). Polarization thus comprises the combination of (1) rising disagreements between large camps in society on a whole set of issues and (2) increasing antipathy between the different camps. The disagreements concern values and policy aims and means, but also what can be considered relevant facts, such as the necessity for rapid and massive reduction of carbon dioxide and methane emissions to mitigate climate change.

Disagreements as such are not a problem because they are part of any pluralistic democratic society: different worldviews and different interests may clash and not all conflicts can be resolved. Yet, polarization, if uncontained, may ultimately tear society apart and damage the legitimacy and effectiveness of the democratic decision-making process, if e.g., the willingness of the minority to accept majority rule or the respect for guaranteeing basic rights to minorities in society can no longer be taken for granted.

The two dimensions of polarization vary in how much they are likely to damage democracy: ideological polarization (increasingly different opinions) may be less harmful than increasing affective polarization.

The introduction of more radical ideas may not necessarily hurt the democratic quality of debates. Sometimes debates lack ideas that are radical, those that get to the roots of a given problem. This is certainly the case for many debates around climate change and the truth does not lie in the middle (anthropogenic climate change *does* exist, and not just a little bit), nor are real solutions to be found in modest, small steps (a bit of climate protection will not be sufficient).

Affective polarization, on the other hand, as in toxic language that hurts an outgroup or is designed to provoke aggression towards an outgroup, can hardly be justified as somehow fostering democracy.

How Does the Media Contribute to Polarization?

Much past research was based on surveys exploring polarization in the minds of people, yet it is also worthwhile to explore how polarization evolves in communication, a concept that I have called "discursive polarization" (Brüggemann and Meyer, 2023). How and why do debates fall apart? This is important because communication (discursive polarization) impacts the minds of people, ultimately resulting in action and — sometimes — even violence.

Political actors who strategically stoke conflict and demonize their opponents for political gain are often the drivers behind the polarization of debates. Yet, in this essay, I will temporarily ignore the Donald Trumps of this world (he is not unique) and instead focus on some of the actors that have contributed to making him and his fellow populists great (again): journalists and social media platform providers. How have they contributed to polarization and could they undo some of it?

The media facilitated Donald Trump's rise by doing what they always do: following their professional or algorithmic logics. It is notable that both news and digital networks push public debates in the same direction: providing most salience to a very limited number of extreme voices engaged in a simplified conflict of pro and con. Conflict, surprise, negativity, and simplicity are factors that have shaped journalistic reporting at least since Walter Lippmann came up with the concept of news value a hundred years ago. In addition, journalistic norms emphasize balance as part of the overarching concept of objectivity, which leads to a search for two dueling sides on every issue and to an overemphasis of fringe statements, e.g., the denial of climate change (Brüggemann and Engesser, 2017).

All this is also due to the market logic of commercial media and the need to maximize audiences by playing into the general psychological dispositions of human attention. Commercial interests have also led to digital platforms to exploit the psychological dispositions of their users. The aim of Facebook and co. seems not so much to benefit users (or society at large) but to trick users into maximizing the amount of time spent on the platform in order to sell targeted advertising, and to collect and sell user data (Zuboff, 2019). Platforms do so by providing content that users "engage" with. This engagement may take the form of reasoned debate but it could also be the exchange of anger or hate speech. This silences moderate voices on social media and leads to news avoidance among parts of the news audience (Bail, 2021).

For those who read social network posts and consume news, they encounter an image of a divided society presented as media content by journalists either claiming that society is increasingly polarized, or by focusing on conflict and negativity and by providing an outlet for extreme fringe voices. This creates a distorted image of society and of the extremeness of the respective outgroup. This distortion is well-documented for the United States, where the public falsely attributes extreme attributes and attitudes to Republican and Democrat partisans (Fernbach and van Boven, 2022).

Could News Media and Digital Platforms Change and Limit Polarization?

So, if all of this is rooted within the DNA of social networks and journalism and ultimately in a commercialized media system and human psychology at large, then there is obviously no simple and quick fix. But is there anything that can be done? Can media change what they do?

Deeper structural reforms of the media system at large (stronger support for public and non-profit media organizations, breaking up giant social media platform providers such as Meta and Alphabet, democratizing media organizations, etc.) would be desirable for less polarized media debates and for better functioning of democracy. Yet, these structural transformations are unlikely to happen soon and are not the focus of this essay. Instead, here, I will provide recommendations for changing media practices that can take place within the context of current media systems.[1]

Even in the current system, news media and platform providers may at some point understand that a good user experience as offered by constructive and inspiring debates about relevant issues may actually also pay off as a business model. Facebook and Twitter are losing users to other platforms, and there might be a chance for new approaches towards creating positive user interactions (although for Twitter, we will have to wait for the demise of Elon Musk). For journalism, change may also be motivated by the desire to do better journalism and to create a community through a positive user experience. Journalism is a practice, a professional culture, that does not change quickly, but can change over time.

Change would have to be driven by management, staff, *and* media users. The fact that the responsibility for fueling the dynamics of polarization is shared does not mean that there is no individual agency. Obviously top management is in a better position to instigate change in hierarchical organizations: digital media platforms and media outlets are not governed democratically and this is part of the problem. So, while it is true that the current platforms and organizations should be democratized, replacing their owners and managers by democratically controlled bodies would solve many problems, but it is not likely to happen any time soon. But media users are super powerful both as subscribers to news media and also as owners of their own time and attention budgets that they might want to spend on a given digital platform. Also, everyone is responsible for which posts they like and circulate: is it a post that spreads contempt towards an outgroup or a constructive idea to address a relevant social problem?

---

1   One may also note that, even among Western countries, media systems vary considerably, e.g., as to their degree of commercialization and the prevalence of hyper-partisan media outlets. Both aspects are likely to enhance polarization. It is plausible that the high degree of polarization in the United States is also (although not exclusively) a result of its hyper-commercialized and partisan media system.

Directions for Change

If we think about a less polarized and less polarizing media debate, media content should obviously not turn a blind eye to problems and conflicts. Yet, reporting and identifying what's wrong in society can only be the starting point for good journalism and debate. Both journalism and social media debates may also provide a perspective on common ground in society, establishing which values, rules, and perceptions of facts are effectively shared. Media professionals can try to refocus debates as a quest for solutions to social problems. More concretely, I would like to make four recommendations.[2]

Firstly, journalists and all professional moderators of media debates could aim *to refocus the public's attention on the bridges that connect a pluralistic society*, e.g., reminding us that virtually everyone agrees on the "if" of climate protection and the debate is only about the "how." Areas of agreement can be explicitly pointed out rather than only highlighting questions of contention. Building bridges also means searching for solutions. Journalism and algorithms may help moderate the search for common ground — but both need reprogramming to do this, which involves changing the routine rules of how they work and what they do. In journalism research, helpful concepts have been developed and applied in practice — such as constructive journalism and solutions journalism — concepts aimed at refocusing reporting on ways out of a given crisis rather than only reporting on the symptoms of the crisis or the most outrageous statements or interactions in a conflict. One important path forward

---

2   The program that I chaired at THE NEW INSTITUTE (Depolarizing Public Debates, Developing the Tools for Transformative Communication) has developed a longer list of recommendations with more elaboration, which has been published as the "Hamburg Impulses" on the website www.transformativecommunication.net. This essay heavily draws on ideas discussed within the program. I would like to thank the members of this program – Hartmut Wessler, Shota Gelovani, Fritz Breithaupt, Ashley Muddiman, Hendrik Meyer, and Louisa Pröschel, as well as short-term visitors Christel von Eck, Dag Elgesem, and Lisa Argyle – for their input into what desirable depolarization is and what could be done to achieve it.

would be to focus more on issues rather than on *who* presented the idea and *how* was it presented. Returning to how disruptive climate protests are covered: reporting and social media have been more focused on the way protesters have protested rather than on their actual propositions (Meyer et al., 2023). Focusing on actual positions reveals that the recent climate protests in Germany organized by the provocatively named Last Generation presented fairly moderate demands.

Secondly, *bridge-builders rather than polarizing figures could be given a voice* in mediated discussions and featured more prominently, e.g., actors that do not clearly reside in a given ideological camp but open up a new perspective or reach out across camps. Interpretive reporting is a journalistic strategy that actively contextualizes fringe voices or even leaves out irrelevant positions, like the denial of basic facts (for an overview of these new role orientations, see Brüggemann, 2017). Polarizing actors are thereby toned down or put into context. This function of journalism is not new: only some voices could be quoted in a traditional newspaper article or on the evening TV news, just as only some Tweets are retweeted a million times. Therefore, the issue is not about silencing voices, but rather deciding the criteria of relevance and making relevant voices more salient.

Thirdly, *aggressive statements by public figures should not be rewarded with media attention*. This runs counter to the journalistic intuition to select issues and statements according to what is likely to draw public attention. Aggression does draw attention — but it is neither always relevant nor helpful in debates that aim to constructively address social problems. Here journalists would have to exercise deliberate constraint.

Social media platforms could retrain their algorithms to search not only for any kind of user activity, but also (and perhaps especially) for constructive dialogue and substantial information. Algorithms can already identify clear cases of incivility (Frimer et al., 2023) and current advances in artificial intelligence suggest that they will be able to discover both constructive interaction and destructive trolling on social media in a much better way in the near future. A deliberativeness algorithm could even moderate discussions and encourage depolarizing exchanges by fostering democratic listening, prompting users to listen and react to the ideas proposed by others (Argyle et al., 2023; Wessler, 2020).

Finally, *debates should not avoid ideas that are radical in the original sense of the word, as in addressing the roots of a problem*, e.g., if the economic system is harmful to democracy or not compatible with the principles of justice and sustainability, then a reformed economic order might be discussed even though it would entail far-reaching changes. This kind of radical idea should not be conflated with an uncivil tone or otherwise extreme positions (in tone or substance) that severely violate basic democracy-sustaining norms. For example, speakers who deny other speakers the right to participate, who do not respect basic rules (such as the results of votes), or those who continuously attack others (verbally or in physical acts of violence) should be toned down.

Let me be clear that depolarizing debates is not about searching for the truth and good ideas only in the middle among those actors who essentially lobby for business as usual and for maintaining the status quo. So-called business-as-usual (BAU) scenarios in climate research have led to disastrous levels of global heating and ecological turmoil. Advocacy for small steps and slow changes is not a moderate proposition, but rather an extreme suggestion given the urgency of climate action. Climate protesters are often labelled as extremists by liberal-conservative actors, but journalists — as the moderators of public debates — should not buy into this discursive strategy and should instead provide fora for debating ideas and solutions. Depolarization strategies are about encouraging unheard voices that are sharing novel ideas rather than those who shout louder and are more offensive than everyone else.

These strategies may help to defuse the destructive dynamics of unconstrained polarization and also make for better journalism and more rewarding experiences for media users. In fact, media users may actually prefer if media debates focused more constructively on solving relevant problems than attacking the other side. It could also be a strategy for countering news avoidance. This could make for a strong argument for media managers and journalists to rethink their current professional practices.

Changing journalistic and media culture is part of the job of journalists and editors, but also of everyone retweeting or liking a post. Every media user may decide to retweet a toxic statement, a cat picture, or an interesting idea addressing relevant social problems. Cat pictures are one way to depolarize public debates but this may not be the most helpful strategy to tackle relevant social problems.

What is considered relevant and what is considered a constructive contribution to public debates is of course a normative question and thus should also be subject to open discussion. If journalists or social media networks choose to intervene to contain polarization, they should be transparent about what they do and why they do so. They will be criticized for this and there will be conflicts — but this is all part of a vibrant democracy. Let the conflict be constructive!

References

Argyle, L. et al. (2023). Leveraging AI for democratic discourse: Chat interventions can improve online political conversations at scale. *Proceedings of the National Academy of Sciences*, 120(41), e2311627120. https://doi.org/10.1073/pnas.2311627120

Bail, C. (2021). *Breaking the Social Media Prism. How to Make Our Platforms Less Polarizing*. Princeton University Press.

Brüggemann, M., & Meyer, H. (2023). When Debates Break Apart: Discursive Polarization as Multi-dimensional Divergence Emerging in and Through Communication. *Communication Theory*, 33(2–3), 132–142. https://doi.org/10.1093/ct/qtad012

Brüggemann, M. (2017). Post-normal Journalism: Climate Journalism and its Changing Contribution to an Unsustainable Debate. In P. Berglez, U. Olausson, & M. Ots (Eds.), *What is Sustainable Journalism? Integrating the Environmental, Social, and Economic Challenges of Journalism* (pp. 57–73). Peter Lang.

Brüggemann, M., & Engesser, S. (2017). Beyond False Balance. How Interpretive Journalism Shapes Media Coverage of Climate Change. *Global Environmental Change*, 42, 58–67. https://doi.org/10.1016/j.gloenvcha.2016.11.004

Fernbach, P. M., & van Boven, L. (2022). False Polarization: Cognitive Mechanisms and Potential Solutions. *Current Opinion in Psychology*, 43, 1–6. https://doi.org/10.1016/j.copsyc.2021.06.005

Frimer, J. et al. (2023). Incivility is Rising Among American Politicians on Twitter. *Social Psychological and Personality Science*, 14(2), 259–269. https://doi.org/10.1177/19485506221083811

Kubin, E., & Sikorski, C. (2021). The role of (social) media in political polarization: A systematic review. *Annals of the International Communication Association*, 45(3), 188–206. https://doi.org/10.1080/23808985.2021.1976070

Lippmann, W. (1997). *Public Opinion*. Macmillan. (Original work published 1922). Available online at http://www.gutenberg.org/etext/6456

Meyer, H., Rauxloh, H., Farjam, M., & Brüggemann, M. (2023). From Disruptive Protests to Discursive Polarization? Comparing German News on Fridays for Future and Letzte Generation. OSF Preprints. https://doi.org/10.31219/osf.io/jkaw8

UNESCO. (2023). *Building Peace in the Minds of Men and Women*. https://en.unesco.org/70years/building_peace

Wessler, H. (2020). Constructive Engagement across Deep Divides. What It Entails and How it Changes Our Role as Communication Scholars. In M. Powers & A. Russell (Eds.), *Rethinking Media Research for Changing Societies* (pp. 139–152). Cambridge University Press.

Wilson, A. E., Parker, V. A., & Feinberg, M. (2020). Polarization in the Contemporary Political and Media Landscape. *Current Opinion in Behavioral Sciences*, 34, 223–228. https://doi.org/10.1016/j.cobeha.2020.07.005

Zuboff, S. (2019). *The Age of Surveillance Capitalism: The Fight for the Future at the New Frontier of Power*. Profile Books.

UNIVERSITIES AS TRUTHSAYERS

JOHN AUBREY DOUGLASS

With the rise of neo-nationalist movements and a global trend toward autocratic-leaning governments, how might universities innovate to be more engaged and influential in combating attacks on open societies and, more generally, promote functional democracies?

In briefly exploring this topic, it is important to note that universities operating in liberal democracies, even those under threat, have much more leeway to affect change than, say, universities that are struggling to operate in increasingly authoritarian nation-states — a topic I have explored in previous writings.[1] For this reason, I focus this short essay on the realm of functioning democracies, with all their flaws and weaknesses.

---

1 See John Aubrey Douglass, *Neo-Nationalism and Universities: Populists, Autocrats, and the Future of Higher Education*, Johns Hopkins University Press, Open Access Project Muse, 2021. See also, What is the fate of Hong Kong's universities under Xi?, *University World News*, November 3, 2021; What's New About Neo-Nationalism? Autocrats Are Ancient. But Globalization, Migration, and Technology Are Giving Them Fresh Power, *Zocalo Public Square*, December 13, 2021; Under attack: universities and neo-nationalist movements, *University World News*, September 4, 2021; A Bolsonaro defeat will not fully undo his damage to Brazilian science: Deep cuts may be reversed, but the Brazilian president's anti-science rhetoric will do lasting damage, *Times Higher Education*, December 10, 2021; How Will "Benedict" Trump Be Remembered? The January 6 Coup Attempt in Historical Perspective, *LA Progressive*, February 3, 2022.

Within liberal democracies, universities act as anchor institutions with a breadth of influence unique within nation-states. But they are also viewed by many as elite enterprises, sometimes reinforcing inequality and acting as tools of globalists who ignore the wants and problems of local communities in a callous quest for open markets and international networks. More specifically, populist and neo-nationalist political actors espouse the view of universities as influential cogs in the so-called sinister "deep-state", as illiberal public spaces, intolerant of dissenting opinions, and increasingly dominated by largely left-wing actors — a view held with significant nuance even among those of moderate political persuasions and affiliations.

Part of the problem is within the academy itself, which often undervalues local engagement. In some instances, the academic community has also shifted increasingly toward liberal litmus tests and reactive responses to radical right criticisms and political power, furthering the political and identity tribalism that erodes broad notions of democratic values. From cancel culture to the concept of gender fluidity, and sometimes extremely broad hate speech or so-called "trigger" speech policies — we can argue about what is anecdotal and what is truly problematic. We can say that the more negative perceptions of academics and universities amplified by largely right-wing media and social networks are not entirely inaccurate and, more importantly, pose a problem of eroding credibility with the larger public.

There is more. The tragedy of the Hamas/Gaza/Israel war has resulted in an unprecedented tumult of opposing demonstrators on many major university campuses in the US and Europe. Irreconcilable pro-Israel and pro-Palestinian views have led to counter demonstrations, pitting student against student and faculty and staff against their counterparts, and generating a reductionist and often destructive campus environment, drowning out those who might simply argue for an end to the war and for peace, and who find fault with all warring parties committing mass murder. The mantra "give peace a chance" is lost to historical memory amid violent clashes, the use of social media to promote disinformation, the formation of often leadership-less demonstrations, hateful doxing, and the like. The social activism promoted by universities has seemingly digressed into open intolerance.

Particularly in the US, but also in the EU, the uncivil nature of this debate creates one more real and exaggerated view of universities as intolerant environments — even if the most politically active and vocal are a minority in the larger academic community. Intolerance is a theme happily amplified in the right-wing media and politicking government hearings, adding to what could be viewed as an unprecedented credibility gap for universities, and their academic leaders, that will take years to hopefully repair.

As of this writing, there is also growing evidence of what might be called a Neo-Academic Cold War, the result of growing global economic and technological competition, and geo-political tensions. China's rise and military ambitions, and soft and sharp power agenda, Russia's unjustified war on Ukraine, political realignments reminiscent but different from the first Cold War; all have had a consequential impact on universities. After a period of integration, we now have a world of escalating economic sanctions, visa restrictions, war, and failed state-driven diasporas, as well as concerns over economic, political, and academic espionage and subterfuge.

Against these headwinds, we should all hope that universities can play an essential and elevated role in supporting open societies and democracies. Further, that the scientific knowledge and other forms of new knowledge they generate can drive or at least shape responsible public discourse on such important issues as climate change, clean energy and sustainability, pandemics, poverty, racism, immigration, the impact of technology, and, more generally, the promotion of rational thinking and policymaking.

Over decades, political observers have extolled the power not only of rational thinking, but also of competent communication to bring about mutual understanding and constructive social change. Never mind for now the many evils of social media and state-controlled narratives that supply Orwellian untruths practiced by Donald Trump, Viktor Orbán, Vladimir Putin, Jinping Xi and other demagogues and autocrats; the concept of free and open communication as a mainstay for old and new democracies remains relevant.

If we adhere to this idea and hope that universities are important sources of truth and knowledge, as well as civil discourse, then, as noted, they need to seek ways to increase their credibility and expand their role in and influence on society. Sticking to a fanciful vision of the academy as exclusively an autonomous ivory tower separated from the society it serves is old-school thinking. Universities can retain that role, but they also need a larger vision to shape public discourse, even if it might at times infringe on their non-partisan ethos.

Shifting the internal culture of universities, and mitigating these perceptions, is a large-scale challenge and a long-term project. My view is that universities need to innovate and do more to support democracies and to resurrect their credibility. But how?

Pathways of Influence

To state the obvious, the role of universities in society and their level of autonomy are largely subjugated to the national political world they operate in. That role is conditioned by what might be termed the indicators or values of healthy democracies, including equitable and impartial rule of law and explicit civil rights, a free *and* responsible news and media sector, an independent civil society, fair elections, stable economies, and trusted governments and public institutions.

A university can be both a vital player as well as an influencer in the vitality of democracies. Yet it is important to note that these institutions in themselves cannot offer a magic bullet to sustain, or restore, or reinvent functioning democracies. Their role is nuanced and multiple. (Let's ignore for now historical instances of universities as catalysts and centers for resistance against autocratic governments — roles that may be more difficult to replicate in the age of the autocratic technological surveillance state.)

Those realities noted, within liberal democracies there are numerous paths for universities to elevate their constructive role in supporting and promoting open societies and democracy. They can do better at educating future citizens and leaders about the value and mechanisms of healthy democracies; they can more clearly voice their role as open markets for political and social ideas, and pursue policies for that cause; they can increase their output of research and knowledge production that is relevant to local communities, from scientific exploration of the local impact of climate change and studies to mitigate socioeconomic disparities, to the history and culture of a region.

Universities can also seek to expand public service engagement including ways to better support public institutions and services, and, one hopes, their efficiency and credibility; they can become more active players in life-long learning and other forms of educational services that meet public needs and expand their networks and influence.

These institutions also offer paths for international engagement and networks that can help local communities better understand the larger world, value cultural diversity, and, in some instances, help meet local labor and other economic needs. Universities also play an increasingly important role in promoting regional economic health. Historically, the collapse of economies, or severe economic dislocation for sizable portions of a nation's population, has provided the pre-conditions for fascism and other forms of autocratic rule — part of the formula for nationalism gone haywire (Galston and Kamarck, 2022). In their book *Why Nations Fail*, Daron Acemoglu and James Robinson outline this relationship between economic prosperity and political accountability (Acemoglu and Robinson, 2012).

Universities can and should be paths for socioeconomic mobility, for easing income inequality; they act as producers of educated citizens, skilled labor, and new knowledge that supports economic growth and competent governments; they act as a constructive social critic important for maintaining political accountability. No other institution, public or private, plays such a multifaceted and critical role for democratic societies. Global challenges almost always have a local dimension. Here lies a pathway for universities.

Finally, academic communities can and often do provide constructive criticism of society and political actors and their policies. They can function as "truthsayers" that confront or at least attempt to expose the dangerous rhetoric of populists and demagogues and their followers who seek to erode democratic societies. More generally, academic communities can provide nuance and insight around the challenges facing society. This is a critical role, whether it pertains to relatively healthy liberal democracies or to democracies threatening to slide toward more autocratic regimes, as well as to actual autocracies — while recognizing the limits of this role when faced with nascent and fully blown security states.

It is important to note that vibrant open societies are not only dependent on institutional mechanisms and agents, like free elections, the rule of law, and courts that uphold civil liberties; they are also dependent on a culture of participatory citizenship, of tolerance and inclusion, and a semblance of socioeconomic equality and opportunity. Within this broader concept, contemporary universities are unique institutions due to the variety of ways they can constructively promote democracies and civil society — although admittedly with occasional complicated political consequences and demands for financial resources.

I like to say that those universities that see themselves as leading regional and national institutions should contemplate how, in some way, they can positively impact the life of every citizen, whether in a region, state, or nation, or some other definition of their stakeholders and the communities they are intended to serve.

For brevity, here I focus on two "interventions": expanding the research and knowledge production portfolio of universities, and the need to vastly improve communication and, one hopes, persuasion and legitimacy in shaping public discourse and policy. The goal is to urge universities to become more impactful and visible institutions, and to improve public discourse. This is no easy task. The reality is that universities, perhaps like other examples of proposed sites of intervention in this book, have limited ways to directly or immediately positively impact democracies: there can only be multiple and holistic approaches that are long-term projects.

Research for the Public Good

Universities need to coherently and purposefully expand research and outreach that benefits economic and social prosperity within a geographic area that constitutes its constituency. Many universities are doing this in some form, but not with enough focus, and with limited concepts of socioeconomic engagement.

As noted previously, one obstacle is an internal academic culture that undervalues local engagement. Overwhelmed by the mantra of global rankings and international citation indexes as indicators of quality, universities and their academic communities need a partial pivot to improve their local impact and profile. University hiring and advancement policies and practices need to place greater value on research focused on local and regional challenges. These often relate to global challenges articulated in the UN's Sustainable Development Goals that could be applied at the local level, although obviously not exclusively.

In addition to the deleterious impact of rankings and their progeny, the "World Class University" model, another feature of academic culture is the historical importance of university autonomy from the political and economic world that surrounds them. There has been much consternation about utilitarian views and the entanglements presented by greater engagement with society. But it is simply not an either-or conundrum; with proper governance structures, internal policies and behaviors, universities can expand their impact judiciously.

More specifically, universities need to develop policies and practices that give greater clarity to the roles and expectations of faculty in meeting the university's mission. Any credible effort requires a process of faculty-driven pre- and post-tenure peer review, and should not be based on a civil service mentality in which faculty advancement is largely a factor of seniority. It also requires a nuanced understanding and validation of research activity, including the concept of engaged scholarship.

Hiring and promotion also needs to focus on a record and promise of creativity and innovation — not simply quantity. This means altering a culture fixated in a narrow concept of economic impact tied to citation rankings. Within a research university, faculty activity can be conceptualized in eight areas: teaching, mentoring, research, academic entrepreneurship, professional competence, professional activity, university service, and public service or engagement. Theoretically, the weighting will vary depending on faculty members' disciplines, interests, abilities, and the stage of their academic careers.

Shaping faculty behavior requires a significant institutional effort and a culture of self-improvement among academics that values public engagement in a variety of forms. It means resisting the reductionist focus on citations currently promoted by university leadership as well as governments in the quest for better commercial rankings. The gist is that in many universities there is a misalignment of the mission and internal culture of faculty and researchers that needs to be addressed to better promote the societies they are intended to serve.

Universities also need to think more systematically about their communication strategies and their powers of persuasion. An obvious task is to formulate with more clarity who the stakeholders are for a university and the communities they wish to help and speak to, whether in Hamburg or Berkeley.

One way to do this is a greater integration of local academics and university staff into local media, government proceedings, and public events that encourage dialogue. Here they can translate research, scientific findings, knowledge, and resources to local needs and concerns. At the same time, faculty, and universities more generally, need to carefully balance their roles as researchers and creators of knowledge and expertise with their potential role as political advocates.

Universities also need to have both campus-wide and discipline-based (e.g., medical centers) communication plans supported by professional staff, some of whom focus on government relations and integrating academic research into local and national policy discussions, others on internal university communications. Such communication plans should always include alumni relations and an understanding that students are tremendously important for leveraging support for universities and elevating their credibility via curricular innovations like service-learning courses and student volunteering and internships in local government, schools, and the private sector.

Some academics have good instincts for making their research understandable to the public, but many do not. And many need encouragement and assistance. THE NEW INSTITUTE's Founding Director Wilhelm Krull and his colleague Thomas Brunotte observe that "universities are still committed to a linear sender-receiver model of communications," and advocate that "an open dialogue replace the traditional monologue" (Krull and Brunotte, 2021).

How well or how poorly academics communicate with the larger world was the subject of a study published by the National Academy of Sciences in the US. In short, universities need a greater understanding and appreciation for why some people are "anti-science" and distrust public institutions (Philipp-Muller et al., 2022). The report states that universities should focus more of their research efforts and services (like consulting with local governments) on topics that are directly relevant to local and regional communities; further, that local academic actors, including faculty and graduate students who live in and are part of the community, should have greater empathy when engaging with stakeholders.

The National Academy of Sciences report also observes that university actors need to consider the social identities and ways of thinking of the various communities they hope to influence (for example, climate change deniers): there is often a "mismatch between the delivery of the scientific message and the recipient's epistemic style." Academic communities should think in nuanced ways and, frankly, more analytically about their powers of persuasion. As one of the co-authors says, "Pro-science messages can acknowledge that there are valid concerns on the other side but explain why the scientific position is preferable" (ibid.).

Universities, and their academic communities, need to focus some of their efforts on "government relations." This includes engaging directly with lawmakers and government staff, tracking legislation, and seeking paths for lobbying in the halls of government, whether to preserve academic freedom and the autonomy of institutions or to seek funding. Universities in liberal democracies have tended to avoid such proactive strategies, seeing their distance from the political fray as a value that helps preserve their autonomy. But this is increasingly a naive view. To preserve democracy, universities need to be more strategically engaged in the process and to act as influencers. And in doing so, seek to build coalitions of like-minded universities.

The credibility gap that universities face in the modern world has led to a nascent series of ventures. Here I note a few examples.

With repeated political attacks on its autonomy and successive state budget cuts to its campus, the academic leadership at the University of Wisconsin–Madison is seeking a path to "fix its public image" (Knox, 2024). This includes a university conducted survey of how voters view the university, and, in turn, a public campaign intended for Wisconsin voters to counter perceptions that the university is "elitist" and insular — in part to demonstrate the multiple ways that university research and students are engaged in community efforts to manage climate change, expand health care services, and the like.

At my university, the University of California, Berkeley, there are initiatives and programs that engage government partners, community leaders, and citizens in the pursuit of formulating largely local policies related to climate change, healthcare, voting participation, housing, violent crime, and other challenges. One example is the "Possibility Lab" that organizes interactions with community members in the region and compiles their concerns and observations to systematically translate them into quantitative measures and policy initiatives. "Communities most directly harmed by broken systems are often left out of conversations about how to make change," explain the project's founding directors. "Developing new ways to ensure communities have a meaningful voice in the policies that affect them can move us towards a more holistic, stakeholder-engaged reimagining of our public systems." The title of two of the lab's projects indicates the breadth of its agenda: Reimagining Public Safety in the City of Oakland and Understanding the Conditions for Success in Permanent Supportive Housing.[2]

At the University of St. Gallen (HSG) in Switzerland, a privately financed building called SQUARE is a self-titled "experiment" to create a "public place for encounters and a forum for dialogue between science, society, business, politics, and culture". Opened in early 2022, the objective is to gather "outstanding minds from business, politics and culture [to] meet students, lecturers and HSG alumni. In the 21st century, ideas and innovations are created in teams, at the interface of different perspectives, interests and biographies."[3]

---

2   For more information on UC Berkeley's Possibility Lab and how it is encouraging democracy, see its website: https://possibilitylab.berkeley.edu/our-work/initiatives/

3   For more information on SQAURE, see the website: https://www.unisg.ch/en/newsdetail/news/square-the-newest-building-at-the-university-of-stgallen-where-the-future-of-learning-and-teaching-is-explored/

Admittedly, reaching out and finding productive ways to engage with disaffected communities, such as conservatives who doubt the reality of climate change, is a more difficult challenge. The argument here is that universities need to become more systematic in their efforts to positively influence society and to elevate their credibility as they face an increasingly cynical view of their place in society.

A "Truthsayer" Role

Yet universities cannot be all things to all people. As I've indicated, their power of persuasion has limits. Hard-core extremists on the left and the right, for example, have world views that are largely unshakable in the near-term and perhaps even in the long-term. This is not to diminish the critical role of universities as truthsayers. Through research and advocacy, universities can and do play a vital role in contradicting or correcting gross mistruths or even nuanced lies and false claims that are damaging to democracies.

This is not an easy task in a world of false narratives that will only increase with advances in AI and increasingly sophisticated deepfakes. Indeed, understanding the past and future impact of social media and technologies such as AI is a major challenge for society.

At the same time, the viability of the truthsayer role relies on an expanded portfolio of engagement with society and on the credibility of the academic community with the public. Academic communities need to work harder to be overtly and visibly inclusive public squares for constructive debate via public events and through their teaching and research programs. Messaging this mission to the public needs to be a central tenant.

While I have focused here on local engagement and skills of constructive communication, I do not mean to downplay the role of universities as sanctuaries for "blue-sky research" untethered by the wants and demands of a larger world. Nor as participants in what is an evolving global science and knowledge system. They are important conduits for integrating global perspectives at the local level. Universities are key players in science diplomacy and in providing contact and support with academics and institutions facing persecution in an increasing number of illiberal democracies and autocratic regimes.

Reflecting geopolitical tensions, we are sliding toward a neo-academic cold war. War, trade sanctions, and new and renewed geopolitical rivalries are shaping how universities interact globally. Universities in the EU have appropriately ended all exchange and research engagements with Russia's universities; China's expanded and severe security state and soft-power efforts abroad, and the fear of academic espionage, is hindering academic collaborations; the wars in Ukraine and in Gaza, and political repression in Hong Kong, Turkey, and elsewhere, are creating a new academic diaspora.

The result of these relatively new tensions is a further divide and isolation of academics caught between rival global players — one leaning autocratic and one that leans toward the values of open societies, with some nations attempting to be neutral or non-aligned. One can only hope that universities in working democracies, as in the past, help to mitigate this trend by fostering open dialogue and academic exchanges; they need to expand their influence and positive impact on their stakeholders. The headwinds are substantial.

Yet, as I have attempted to portray in this essay, no other institution, public or private, plays such a multifaceted and critical role for democratic nation-states as universities. And here lies an important opportunity. They can and must do more.

References

Acemoglu, D., & Robinson, J. (2012). *Why Nations Fail: The Origins of Power, Prosperity, and Poverty*. Crown.

Douglass, J. A. (2023, March 4). New ideas in the face of rankings and "world-class" fatigue. *University World News*.

Douglass, J. A. (Ed.). (2021). *Neo-Nationalism and Universities: Populists, Autocrats, and the Future of Higher Education*. Johns Hopkins University Press, Open Access Project Muse.

Galston W. A., & Kamarck, E. (2022, January 4). Is Democracy Failing and Putting Our Economic System at Risk? Brookings Institute.

Knox, L. (2024, March 19). Can a Marketing Push Solve UW Madison's Political Woes? *Inside Higher Ed*. https://www.insidehighered.com/news/government/state-policy/2024/03/19/uw-madisons-marketing-push-against-politicization

Krull, W. & Brunotte, T. (2021). Turbulent Times: Intellectual and Institutional Challenges for Universities in Germany, Hungary, and Poland. In John Aubrey Douglass (Ed.), *Neo-Nationalism and Universities: Populists, Autocrats, and the Future of Higher Education*, Johns Hopkins University Press, Open Access Project Muse.

Philipp-Muller, A., Petty, R. E., & Lee, S. W. S. (2022, July 12). Why are people antiscience, and what can we do about it?. Proceedings of the National Academy of Sciences, 119(30). https://doi.org/10.1073/pnas.2120755119

Repucci, S. (2015, August 3). Democracy Is Good for Business. Freedom House.

SOCIALIZATION AS A COUNTER-RIGHT TO DEMOCRATIZE AND RECLAIM THE COMMON

ISABEL FEICHTNER

Social-ecological transformation is the buzzword of the moment. As a lawyer I have long struggled to understand how law might foster a democratic social-ecological transformation; how lawyers might contribute to transformative law. In this endeavor, I find helpful an approach to law that has recently been promoted as "law in political economy." This perspective has its roots in older traditions of legal realism and critical legal studies, and foregrounds law as co-constitutive of political economy and of value-production processes that are often extractive, exploitative, and destructive of life. It can make visible law's implications and complicities and moreover can also draw attention to the potential for transformative experiments through the legal re-design of institutions at the heart of contemporary political economy (Feichtner and Gordon, 2023). It thus points to the potentially transformative role of law in a social-ecological transformation that is radical and not only reformist, that does not content itself with re-regulation or redistribution, but aims at changing and democratizing modes of production and provisioning.

Transformative law that aims at a reconfiguration of political economy so that society's normative objectives, including relational freedom, equitable provisioning, and human as well as non-human flourishing, may be better realized than they are today, should have some idea of the paths and agents of transformation. To enhance the likelihood of contributing to radical transformation, but also to be true to the normative ambitions just mentioned, transformative law should relate to and be informed by social practice and actual political projects by people striving for change (Kennedy, 2016). In this current moment, I consider two projects to be promising in that they point to pathways for radical and radically democratic social-ecological transformation and may provide impulses for a conceptualization of transformative law and a testing ground for transformative legal (and social) experiments. They are projects of commoning and projects of socialization. In the following, I seek to briefly present both projects, to connect commoning to the socialization movement, and to interpret socialization as the exercise of a collective and democratic counter-right directed at the generation of a new common.

Commons and practices of commoning are nothing new: Throughout history, humans all over the world have collectively self-organized in order to build resilient structures for the satisfaction of their material and immaterial needs. Through practices of commoning, commons emerge as social systems around shared, material, and immaterial resources (Hess and Ostrom, 2007; Bollier, 2015). Often commons are associated with precolonial social practices, law, and modes of association, production, and provisioning. Yet many new commons projects are also proliferating — often taking inspiration from and building on older traditions of commoning. Contemporary commons include, e.g., food cooperatives, urban gardening projects, complementary currencies, open-source seeds, and software initiatives. As commons researcher Silke Helfrich used to stress, commons are all around us. We just lack a general language and conceptual frameworks (including legal ones) to recognize and understand them as such.

Contemporary commoning projects and movements that aim for urban and rural, spiritual, cultural, digital, and material commons often respond to financial, economic, ecological, and humanitarian crises. They are driven by a critique of contemporary democratic capitalism and expressions of discontent with individuation; increasing social inequalities; and pervasive processes of economic value production that are extractive and destructive of life. Commons emerge where people collectively self-organize to satisfy their needs and desires equitably, on the basis of relations of solidarity and care, and aimed at furthering aliveness and the "surplus value of lived experience" (Massumi, 2018). They can be considered modes of production, provisioning, and distribution that are complementary to state and market mechanisms. While commons are omnipresent, they can simultaneously be considered radical and revolutionary. They do not offer a blueprint for a different social order. Instead, practices of commoning seek to perform and institute epistemological and ontological shifts and thus reconstitute relations between humans and the non- or more-than-human world. They frequently draw on decolonial knowledges and epistemologies of the Global South to foster their projects of relation-building and world-(re)making. Commoning thus is not a revolution of the kind that overthrows the current system to build a new one on the ruins of the old. Instead, its revolution lies in the reconfiguration of infrastructures and relationality through practice, experimentation, and prefiguration of desired futures.

A question that arises, in particular with a view to the much-needed society-wide "large-scale" social-ecological transformation, is whether commoning — beyond dispersed projects and practices — can generate a new common that may integrate and hold society together. As Bini Adamczak has noted, in contemporary capitalist society it is value production on the basis of private property rights that is "the common" that integrates society in a particular and divisive way: "It is the relationality of value, that creates commonality through individuation, that connects by dividing. It realizes a common privacy and therewith a privatized common. The question that critics of bourgeois society would need to answer is then: What could [...] assume the role that private property plays in bourgeois society. That would be a question concerning relationality" (Adamczak, 2017, my own translation). Contemporary practices of commoning might have the potential to set into motion a relational revolution that replaces this divisive "common privacy" with modes of association and provisioning that connect without dividing and thus generate a new common. As Sabine Hark and her co-authors have noted, "[i]n light of the tendency that the common good merges into market dynamics, the practical experiments of commoning might be seen as attempts to search for new solutions to the unfulfilled promise of a merely abstract claim to universality" (Hark et al., 2015). Commoning may thus be developed into a practice-theory of change — one that in various interconnected projects, in different sectors of society, and at different scales and levels of organization may generate relations, practices, and institutions that prefigure change and prepare a path towards social-ecological transformation.

One project that has particular potential for expanding the commons and fostering a new relational common is socialization, i.e., the transfer of private property to common ownership. Socialization as a project of revolutionary reform (Holm, 2021) gained renewed traction in Germany with the Berlin initiative *Deutsche Wohnen & Co enteignen*. This civil society initiative formed in response to rising rents, gentrification, and expulsions, all of which accelerated due to large-scale privatization of public housing in Berlin in the late 1990s and early 2000s. For the past seven years, the initiative has been successfully organizing around the demand that housing real estate in Berlin owned by large housing companies with portfolios of 3,000 or more apartments be transferred from private property to common ownership through legislation on the basis of Article 15 of the German constitution (the Basic Law). *Deutsche Wohnen & Co enteignen* successfully mobilized for a referendum in which a 57.6% majority voted in favor of such a socialization on September 26, 2021. The referendum mandated the Berlin state government (Senate) to work on legislation that effects such a transfer. In response, the Berlin Senate established an expert commission to examine *inter alia* the legal requirements, in particular of German constitutional law, that socialization would need to meet. I was a member of this commission, which delivered its report to the Berlin Senate on June 28, 2023. The report finds that the socialization of housing real estate in Berlin does not meet any unsurmountable legal obstacles. While the government of Berlin is still not willing to initiate work on a socialization law, public debate and civil society mobilization around socialization has — in the meantime —spread widely, geographically as well as thematically. Mobilization for socialization now extends beyond housing to such social infrastructures such as health, energy, education, and agriculture.

Article 15, the socialization clause of the Basic Law reads: "Land, natural resources and means of production may, for the purpose of socialization, be transferred to common ownership or other forms of a common economy by a law that determines the nature and extent of compensation."[1] To date, however, it has never been put to use. In the current debate, lawyers are proposing two contrasting interpretations of this provision: one that aims for stabilization and another that aims for transformation. On the basis of these divergent interpretations, I wish to clarify my notion of counter-rights and transformative law that make space for the emergence of a new common.

The interpretation that aims at systemic stabilization regards socialization on the basis of Article 15 as an emergency measure to satisfy basic needs when the market economy fails to meet these needs. It understands socialization as a massive infringement of the individual right to private property and therefore demands that socialization meet strict requirements. One of these requirements is proportionality, a legal principle the Federal Constitutional Court of Germany developed in its case law as an unwritten constitutional limitation to state power. Proportionality requires that a measure that infringes on a constitutional right has to pursue a legitimate interest. The measure moreover must be necessary to further this interest, meaning that no less intrusive measure that could do the job is available. And finally, the measure's harmful effects (to the rights-holders) must not outweigh its benefits to society.

Applied to socialization, proportionality strips it of its revolutionary potential. It paves the way for a balancing of interests (and values) within the given systemic framework of contemporary political economy — on the one hand, the interests of private enterprise that are compromised by socialization, on the other, the interest in affordable housing. It opens the door to questions of whether other measures are available to the state

[1] The official translation uses the word nationalization instead of socialization. This is misleading, however, as socialization is not to be confused with a measure that merely transfers ownership of means of production or land to the state without also changing the mode of production and provisioning.

by which it may ensure an adequate supply of affordable housing, such as caps on rents, subsidies, new construction, etc. Proportionality also prompts an inquiry into whether and under what circumstances affordable housing is an objective that is important (or endangered) enough that it justifies the taking of private property on a large scale. In the last step of the proportionality test — the harm-benefit-balancing exercise — the value of housing is then placed on one side of the scale and weighed against the value of private property on the other. Given the high value accorded by proponents of this interpretation to private property, their assessment of its infringement as "massive," and the endless arsenal of alternative policies and regulatory instruments at the state's disposal that appear less intrusive, socialization becomes an emergency measure of last resort. A measure that the state only may resort to if other public welfare means can no longer ensure the level of affordable housing that the state must guarantee under its human rights obligations. I call this interpretation "stabilizing" as it regards the capitalist market economy and a state that extends welfare to those otherwise "left behind" as the desirable status quo and socialization as an instrument that may be used only in the direst of circumstances — ultimately to uphold and stabilize the current political economy.

The transformative interpretation, by contrast, regards Article 15 not as a limitation to the individual right to private property, but understands it as a right itself: not as an individual right that protects against state power, such as the right to private property, but as a democratic right to be exercised collectively, namely by the legislature that passes the socialization law. It is a democratic right, firstly, because it is exercised by the democratically elected state organs. Secondly, Article 15 is a democratic right since the purpose ascribed to it is not the satisfaction of predetermined needs and interests (e.g., affordable housing) or the realization of values enshrined in constitutions and international human rights covenants (e.g., the right to housing) — but rather the democratization of society. If this conception were endorsed, proponents of socialization would neither have to specify the interests and values pursued by socialization nor how these interests, e.g., the interest in affordable housing, are met by a transfer of private property in real estate to common ownership. Socialization would only require a political decision and a legislative act that transfers private property to common ownership and provides just compensation for the previous owners.

This interpretation of Article 15 does not deny that socialization pursues a myriad of public interests. It certainly does — including, but not limited to, expanding the supply of affordable housing, preventing the extraction of rent and of gentrification, and allowing for more control over the administration of housing stock, including the implementation of climate change mitigation and adaptation measures. Yet, focusing merely on the satisfaction of basic needs and the promotion of public interests in a given political economy, i.e., an economy in which land and houses are commodified and assetized, detracts attention from the transformative potential of socialization initiatives. Thus, imagination is foreclosed in regard to what housing might mean if land were commonly owned and the city were reclaimed as a commons.

To emphasize the transformative potential of commoning, I suggest understanding socialization not only as a democratic right, but also as a counter-right. The conception of Article 15 as a counter-right can build on various works in German legal scholarship (Ridder, 1975; Menke, 2015; Teubner, 2020). Accordingly, Article 15 could be understood as a counter-right against the right to private property (as the basis of the divisive common identified by Bini Adamczak) and as a counter-right against the requirement — often imposed in public discourse on those demanding change — to frame affects, emotions, passions, and desires in the terms of interests. According to Gunther Teubner, the "institutional imagination" (Unger, 1996) of collective counter-rights not only serves the development of political programs, but also, and more importantly, collective counter-rights are needed so that "pre-conceptual affection can be articulated within social movements, organizations, associations, labor unions and NGOs, so they can produce collective political judgments in mediation with conceptual determinations" (Teubner, 2020, p. 388). Counter-rights could enlarge "the social spaces for collective will-formation" (ibid.). In the realm of urban real estate, socialization as the exercise of a counter-right would quite literally make space — space for people to meet in new and unpredictable constellations, space in which social movements can form, convene, and cultivate democratic practice.

Such an interpretation of Article 15 of the Basic Law finds support in constitutional history and alternative interpretations of the social state — alternative to the concept of the interventionist and stabilizing welfare state outlined above. Thus, constitutional lawyer Helmut Ridder interpreted the social state objective in the German constitution as demanding a democratization of all spheres of society (not only state institutions). Democratization here means the dismantling of societal relations of power so that the social state is not reduced to a welfare state that is external to society and extends charity to people "left behind," but is rather a state that promotes relational freedom through collective self-organization (Ridder, 1975).

Democratization of society is a demanding concept. Socialization, in the transformative sense of making space for a new common to replace the divisive common of private property, can be the necessary first step but it will not be sufficient on its own. Legal and institutional arrangements will be needed to fill the space and facilitate, promote, and protect collective self-organization for the realization of relational freedom. In this respect, the practice-theory of commons and commoning can provide guidance on which rules, principles, procedures, and patterns (Bollier and Helfrich, 2019) may enable and foster a relationality that is not characterized by domination, but rather by equality, and one that allows for equitable sharing and provisioning that responds to peoples' (changing) needs and desires. Inspiration, e.g., for the question of how common ownership in housing should be (self-)administered, may be drawn from past instances and models of participation — *inter alia* workers' participation (Deutsche Wohnen & Co enteignen, 2023). In order to concretize what future housing commons might look like and what role the state might play after socialization, it seems particularly promising to further develop the concept of Commons-Public Partnerships (Helfrich and Bollier, 2015) as a counter-model to Public-Private Partnerships, and to promote local self-government and the right to the city (Gruber, 2021; Schubel, 2024). It would be one piece in the larger puzzle of a transformative law for the common(s).

References

Adamczak, B. (2017). *Beziehungsweise Revolution. 1917, 1968 und kommende.* Suhrkamp.

Bollier, D. (2015). *Commoning as a Transformative Social Paradigm.* http://www.truevaluemetrics.org/DBpdfs/Initiatives/Next-System-Project/David-Bollier-Commoning-as-a-Transformative-Social-Paradigm.pdf

Bollier, D., & Helfrich, S. (2019). *Free, Fair, and Alive. The Insurgent Power of the Commons.* New Society.

Deutsche Wohnen & Co. enteignen. (2023). Gemeingut Wohnen. Eine Anstalt öffentlichen Rechts für Berlins vergesellschaftete Wohnungsbestände. https://content.dwenteignen.de/uploads/Gemeingut_Wohnen_3a03fa4c87.pdf

Feichtner, I., & Gordon, G. (Eds.). (2023). *Constitutions of Value. Law, Governance and Political Ecology.* Routledge. https://doi.org/10.4324/9781003221920

Gruber, S., (2021). Über die Möglichkeit von Public-Commons-Partnerschaften. Wiens Koproduktion von Wohnraum und das politische Projekt der Stadt, *ARCH+*, 244, 160–165.

Hark, S., Jaeggi, R., Kerner, I., Meißner, H., & Saar, M. (2015). Das umkämpfte Allgemeine und das neue Gemeinsame. *Feministische Studien: Zeitschrift für interdisziplinäre Frauen- und Geschlechterforschung*, 33(1), 99–103. http://dx.doi.org/10.25595/1944

Hess, C., & Ostrom, E. (2006). Introduction: An Overview of the Knowledge Commons. In C. Hess, & E. Ostrom (Eds.), *Understanding Knowledge as a Commons. From Theory to Practice* (pp. 3–26). MIT Press. https://doi.org/10.7551/mitpress/6980.003.0003

Holm, A. (2021). *Objekt der Rendite. Zur Wohnungsfrage und was Engels noch nicht wissen konnte.* Dietz Berlin.

Kennedy, D. (2016). *A World of Struggle. How Power, Law, and Expertise Shape Global Political Economy.* Princeton University Press. https://doi.org/10.2307/j.ctt1wf4cz3

Massumi, B. (2018). 99 *Theses on the Revaluation of Value. A Postcapitalist Manifesto.* University of Minnesota Press.

Menke, C. (2015). *Kritik der Rechte.* Suhrkamp.

Ridder, H. (1975). *Die soziale Ordnung des Grundgesetzes. Leitfaden zu den Grundrechten einer demokratischen Verfassung*. Westdeutscher. https://doi.org/10.1007/978-3-322-84231-2

Schubel, K. (2024). Demokratisierung städtischen Raums: Ein Recht für Urban Commons. In U. Klüh, & R. Sturn (Eds.). *Commons, Jahrbuch Normative und institutionelle Grundlagen der Ökonomik*, 21. Metropolis.

Teubner, G. (2020). Counter-Rights. On the Trans-Subjective Potential of Subjective Rights, In P. F. Kjaer (Ed.). *The Law of Political Economy. Transformation in the Function of Law* (pp. 372–393). Cambridge Univeristy Press. https://doi.org/10.1017/9781108675635.015

Unger, R. M. (1996). Legal Analysis as Institutional Imagination. *Modern Law Review*, 59, 1–23. https://doi.org/10.1111/j.1468-2230.1996.tb02063.x

DETHRONING ELECTIONS: WHY THE FUTURE OF DEMOCRACY REQUIRES NEW WAYS OF PICKING LEADERS

MAX KRAHÉ

In our times, elections are near-synonymous with democracy. This is new — and dangerous. Resisting oligarchic drift requires new approaches to picking our political leaders.

Why? By their very nature, elections divide. Not just Team Red from Team Blue or Team Left from Team Right but, more fundamentally, protagonists from the chorus, actors from the spectators, a field of the few from an electorate of the many. All the attention they whip up, all the excitement they generate gets channeled away from the people and onto the candidates who strut on the stage. Their essence, in other words, is distinction (Manin, 1997).

This distinction is not innocent. In drawing it, elections create a hierarchy and call it a demos. Worse, still, is the ethos they create: celebrity culture and subservience, hyperactivity and paralysis, apathy and rage. Counterintuitive as it may sound, elections corrupt democracy.

For most of written history, random selection (also known as sortition) was the default mechanism for filling offices in a democracy (Sintomer, 2023). In Ancient Athens, for example, nearly all offices — legislative, executive, and in the judiciary — were filled by lot.

This was common sense. Aristotle declared "the appointment of magistrates by lot is thought to be democratic, and the election of them oligarchical" (Aristotle, 350 B.C.E./1885, *Politics*, Book IV, chapter 9, 1294b7-9). Two thousand years later, little had changed: in 1748, Montesquieu wrote "choosing by lot is in the nature of democracy; choosing by vote is in the nature of aristocracy" (Montesquieu, 1748/1989, Book 2, chapter 2, p. 13).

Yet today, we conflate democracy with elections. Why? What happened after 1748? How did elections push aside sortition?

To understand this transformation, we must return to the 18th century and the Atlantic Revolutions. These uprisings, and the American and the French Revolutions in particular, were rebellions against absolutism and arbitrary rule. To replace King George III and the ancien régime, however, their leaders chose a system called representative government. This was distinct from and in opposition to democracy (Manin, 1997). Democracy was about equal political power and equality between rulers and the ruled. Representative government was about selecting capable rulers and restraining them through trial by discussion.

Why this choice? Three arguments swayed the revolutionaries. First, leading voices argued that "we should be governed by the best" (Boissy d'Anglas, cited in Van Reybrouk, 2016, p. 59). While they fought against feckless kings, lords, and barons, many of the revolutionaries believed in the existence of a *natural* aristocracy: excellent citizens with superior talent, skills, and knowledge. According to Jefferson and others, these "natural *aristoi*" should steer the ship of state (Jefferson, 1813). Elections would pick them out and put them at the helm. Selection by lot would not.

A second argument was inspired by thinkers like Machiavelli and Hobbes, keen observers of power. Social and economic elites tend to develop political ambitions, too, they noted. Sortition would frustrate those ambitions because it blocks wealth and prestige from translating into office. Elections, in contrast, are won with money and social standing. This turns them into lightning rods, channeling the burning ambitions of elites into law-abiding competition and away from coups or other extra-constitutional schemes.

Finally, many of the revolutionaries were outright skeptical of democracy. James Madison, for example, saw democracies as "spectacles of turbulence and contention, ... as short in their lives as they have been violent in their deaths" (Madison, 1788/2008, p. 52). John Adams exclaimed "There never was a democracy yet that did not commit suicide" (Adams, 1851, p. 484). Even Rousseau wrote "there is no government as subject to civil wars and intestine turmoil as democratic or popular government" (Rousseau, 1762/1997, Book III, chapter 4, p. 92). These were echoes of old fears: From Plato to Hannah Arendt, a certain kind of philosopher has always worried that democracy degenerates into mob rule. Socrates, after all, was executed by Athenian democracy.

It was not just a fear of instability that predisposed the revolutionaries against democracy. Many of them were rich — and democracy was seen as a direct threat to that wealth. For Madison, democracy was "incompatible with personal security or the rights of property" (Madison, 1788/2008, p. 52). Benjamin Constant, author, politician, and participant in the French Revolution, argued "Property must be in charge or annihilated" (Constant, 1810/2003, Book X, chapter 4, p. 169). Wealthy himself, he favored the former.

The 18th-century revolutionaries were thus doubly skeptical about democracy, fearing its effects on both property and stability. At the same time, they took notice of the egalitarian spirit of their times. This made elections the perfect solution: they involved the many but did not give them power. Even under universal suffrage, it is the few who tend to get elected.

These arguments are not without merit. Democracy does have its dangers. They must not blind us, however, to the anti-democratic spirit of elections.

Yes, elections are meant to select for individual ability, to pick out the "natural *aristoi*." However, even if they did so — and whether they do so in practice remains unclear — individual ability may not be the right selection criterion in the first place. Hélène Landemore and others have shown that, when it comes to collective decision-making, diversity often trumps ability. Especially when the range of problems is wide and unpredictable, as it always is in politics, it is "better to have a group of cognitively diverse people than a group of very smart people who think alike" (Landemore, 2012, p. 103). Collective wisdom beats individual ability.

In practice, moreover, elections select for background, not just skills. In the US, political scientists speak of "White-Collar government"; in the Netherlands, of "Diploma Democracy"; in Germany, of government by "[n]one of us." Everywhere across the West, the half that does not go to university is largely excluded from elected office.

If the actions of the elected furthered the interests of the excluded, this might be acceptable. But as recent research has shown for the United States (Gilens and Page, 2014) and Germany (Elsässer et al., 2021), they do not. In both countries, the views of those around the median income seem to have no independent impact on which laws are passed or rejected.

In addition to the misrepresentations they produce, it is also the psychology of elections that corrupts our democracies. Instead of fostering deliberation and disinterested choice, as many had hoped for in the 18th century, we now know that elections lead to *apathy*, *pride*, and *rage*: apathy among those who think their votes don't matter; pride among voters on the winning side; rage among the losers.

This is no coincidence: leaders have good reason to stir up these emotions. The problem that leaders face is that individual votes are statistically insignificant. This makes getting their voters to the polls a perennial challenge. To drive up turnout, it is useful to excite the reptilian parts of our brains. This generates energy, to be sure, but energy that quickly shades into pride or rage.

Further, the same leaders often aim to cultivate apathy, to depress opposition turnout among the electorate of their opponents. None other than Angela Merkel was a master of this strategy: Both her most famous election poster, an image of her trade-mark diamond-shaped hand gesture, and her best-known election slogan, "you know me" (*Sie kennen mich*), were bland, apolitical, and aimed at producing "asymmetric demobilization."

In their psychological effects on candidates, elections are problematic, too. Those who lose may feel snubbed. Their ambition, instead of remaining channeled into regime-internal competition, may strike against

---

1   Asymmetric demobilization was identified in 2009 as a deliberate electoral strategy used by Chancellor Merkel by the economists and political scientists Matthias Jung, Yvonne Schroth, and Andreas Wolf. Since then, the term has entered wide circulation in German political analysis. (Jung, M., Schroth, Y., & Wolf, A. (2009). Regierungswechsel ohne Wechselstimmung. *Aus Politik und Zeitgeschichte*, 51, 12–19.)

the constitutional order itself — whether on January 6th in Washington or January 8th in Brasília. Just as dangerously, elections can seduce their winners into believing they are better than their competitors or, more insidiously, better than the electorate.

Through this, elections open a void between politicians "above" and voters "below" (Mair, 2013). From below, citizens can feel ignored, belittled, and misled. Voters lose trust in politicians. From above, elected officials begin to think of themselves as different from the electorate, as better educated, more open-minded, morally superior (Van Reybrouk, 2016, p. 10). They start to consider themselves a special breed, willing to work the long evenings, to go the extra mile, to shoulder the heavy responsibility, because — and here we circle back to Aristotle and Montesquieu — nobility obliges (*noblesse oblige*).

When this void grows too wide, the distinction too sharp, the corruption of democracy takes a final turn. "Take back control," the sirens start to sing. But in an election-centric system, even this distress call will be dysfunctional. To maximize electoral rewards, the false tribunes of the people will dismiss diversity, deny the existence of trade-offs, and refuse to abide by the informal norms essential to any system of good government.

Perhaps I am exaggerating. Don't elections tie politicians to their voters, anchoring power among the people? How can we *really* know whether elections corrupt democracy?

Observing the distribution of power is hard. Constitutional forms can be deceiving. In any society there are norms and traditions, informal and extra-political resources, hidden connections and cliques. These affect the real distribution of power, sometimes greatly. One of the hallmarks of true power is the ability to remain invisible, when desired.

To cut through this fog, I propose an analytic shortcut. Assume a fundamental human desire for recognition, i.e., to be recognized as (at least) an equal by others of (at least) equal status. Assume also that this recognition has a material element: wealth and income as rough proxies for recognition. These two assumptions allow an inference from equality of social and material conditions to the "democraticity" of regimes. This inference works because, where social and material conditions are very unequal, but the desire for recognition is widespread, power must be concentrated. Otherwise those at the receiving end of inequality would use their share of power to obtain the recognition they desire.

This heuristic is not always accurate. Social and material equality can result from natural catastrophes, pandemics, or wars, not just from an equality of political power (Scheidel, 2017). One can also imagine regimes where power *is* equally distributed, but majorities accept social and economic inequality. Stranger things have happened. Nevertheless, this mental shortcut places the burden of proof appropriately: equal societies receive the benefit of the doubt, stratified ones must prove that their democracy is real.

Using this analytical lens and the evidence of social, material, and political inequality across the West today (Elsässer and Schäfer, 2023), I am not convinced that Western election-centric regimes are full democracies today. As Hélène Landemore has said: "many of the regimes we call representative democracies are hardly democracies in the genuine sense of the term"; they "are de facto usurping the term" (Landemore, 2020, p. 19).

Of course, elections are not the sole cause of inequality. Our politics suffer from "aristocratic excess" (Thompson, 2022, p. 185) for other reasons, too. But our elected governments *accept* inequality. Indeed, the economic policies they pursue often further it. *This* reveals the corruption that elections cause.

If elections corrupt democracy, what is to be done? How should we organize our politics instead?

Direct democracy is not the answer. It has a valuable role to play in certain times and places, but attempted at scale, it takes too many evenings and produces too few results. Politics is labor, and this labor should be divided.

How? This is, above all, a matter for experimentation. Experimentation is not just helpful to discover new democratic forms and processes, but also to keep the future open — itself a key feature of a vibrant, meaningful democracy.

An openness to institutional experimentation must be combined with an openness to geographic, ethnic, and wider epistemological diversity. I am a white man familiar with Western Europe and the United States.

My perspective — both on why elections corrupt and on what should be done in response — is limited. Engaging with other perspectives is essential to render experimentation truly democratic.

But experimentation needs to start with something. Drawing on historical experience and contemporary experiments, both in the Global North and the Global South, sortition is an obvious candidate for this (Bagg, 2024). It confers neither special dignity on winners, nor disdain on those who lose. In spirit, as well as in results, sortition is truly egalitarian, genuinely democratic, and, if carefully designed, statistically representative. It is the prime candidate to dethrone elections.

Of course, sortition is not a panacea (Grandjean et al., 2024). Politics is not just about equality and representation. It is also about expertise and accountability, dimensions on which selection by lot scores poorly. Moreover, randomly selected politicians, whether in the legislature or the executive, risk being outsmarted or dominated by lifelong professionals, whether in political parties, the civil service, or in other expert roles.

Which offices should be filled by sortition requires careful thought, ex ante, and clear-eyed evaluation, ex post. Selection by lot could be tempered by scrutiny, either ex post, where those selected must defend their actions after their term ends, or on an ex-ante or ongoing basis, where lottery candidates must present themselves before juries of their peers. Political parties, too, could continue to play important roles, whether in scrutinizing the selected, training them, or linking them and their deliberations to the process of political will-formation in society at large.

In a spirit of experimentation, combinations of sortition and election could be explored. A new bicameralism could be explored, for example, where a sortition chamber co-legislates with an elected chamber. This could suit unitary states, like France or the Philippines, where a sortition chamber need not compete with the need for federal representation.

The arc of history is already bending in this direction. Experimentation is happening from Finland to South Korea, from Brazil to Belgium. What is clear is that sortition cannot succeed as a mere technical-democratic fix. On their face, laws and decrees are nothing but words. Layered on top of inegalitarian societies, the politics of sortition may itself be corrupted, or trigger elite treason. Equally, without the provision of childcare, appropriate payment for office holders, and limits to wider economic insecurity, sortition itself may become exclusive, open only to those with means.

Democratization and experimentation must therefore extend into the economic sphere, whether through taxation, cooperatives, financial reform, permanent full employment, or commoning. It must also reach into the socio-cultural sphere, for example through practices that develop democratic norms and dispositions, like the art of association, or through amplifying values like faith and courage. Even then, the thorny question remains of whether, once the lottery has spoken, the acceptance of nomination should be voluntary, compulsory, or, most likely, some hybrid of the two. Here, too, experimentation is necessary.

To be successful, the dethroning of elections must be an inclusive project, advanced by broad social movements, not a narrow, technical project, carried by a vanguard or counter-elite alone. None of this is easy. But social, economic, and political change becomes even harder if we misunderstand which parts of our constitutions favor it, and which ones hold it back. Such a misunderstanding surrounds the role and nature of elections today. They are oligarchic, not democratic; corrupting, not constituting democracy. If we want a better future, we should stop worshipping them.

References

Adams, J. (1851). Letter from John Adams to John Taylor, April 15, 1814. In C. F. Adams (Ed.), *The Collected Works of John Adams*, vol. VI. Little and Brown, 1851.

Aristotle. (1885). *Politics* (B. Jowett, Trans.). https://classics.mit.edu/Aristotle/politics.4.four.html (Original work published c. 350 B.C.E.)

Bagg, S. (2024). Sortition as Anti-Corruption: Popular Oversight against Elite Capture. *American Journal of Political Science*, 68(1), 93–105.

Constant, B. (2003). *Principles of Politics* (E. Hofmann, Ed.; D. O'Keeffe, Trans.). Liberty Fund. (Original work published 1810)

Elsässer, L., Hense, S., & Schäfer, A. (2021). Not Just Money: Unequal Responsiveness in Egalitarian Democracies. *Journal of European Public Policy*, 28(12), 1890–1908.

Elsässer, L., & Schäfer, A. (2023). Political Inequality in Rich Democracies. *Annual Review of Political Science*, 26, 469–487.

Gilens, M., & Page, B. I. (2014). Testing Theories of American Politics: Elites, Interest Groups, and Average Citizens. *Perspectives on Politics*, 12(3), 564–581.

Grandjean, G. (Ed.). (2024). *Against Sortition?* Imprinte Academic.

Jefferson, T. (1813). Letter from Thomas Jefferson to John Adams, October, 28, 1813, p. 2, Washington, D.C., Library of Congress, Series 1: General Correspondence, 1651–1827, Microfilm Reel: 046. Available online at http://hdl.loc.gov/loc.mss/mtj.mtjbib021548

Landemore, H. (2020). *Open Democracy: Reinventing Popular Rule for the Twenty-First Century*. Princeton University Press.

Landemore, H. (2012). *Democratic Reason*. Princeton University Press.

Madison, J. (2008). Federalist 10. The Size and Variety of the Union as a Check on Faction. In A. Hamilton, J. Madison, & J. Jay, *The Federalist Papers* (L. Goldman, Ed.). Oxford University Press. (Original work published 1788)

Mair, P. (2013). *Ruling the Void: The Hollowing of Western Democracy*. Verso.

Manin, B. (1997). *The Principles of Representative Government*. Cambridge University Press.

Montesquieu. (1989). *The Spirit of the Laws* (M. Cohler, B. C. Miller, & H. S. Stone, Eds.). Cambridge University Press. (Original work published 1748)

Rousseau, J. J. (1997). *The Social Contract* (V. Gourevitch, Ed.). Cambridge University Press. (Original work published 1762)

Sintomer, Y. (2023). *The Government of Chance: Sortition and Democracy from Athens to the Present*. Cambridge University Press.

Van Reybrouck, D. (2016). *Against Elections: The Case for Democracy* (L. Waters, Trans.). Bodley Head.

INSTRUCTING OUR REPRESENTATIVES: AN ARGUMENT IN FAVOR OF THE IMPERATIVE MANDATE

BRUNO LEIPOLD

Politicians lie. Politicians lie *all the time*. They make promises during elections knowing full well that they will not keep them. They lie in office knowing that there is nothing we can do to remove them until the next election. When they don't lie and genuinely believe what they say, the power of money and corporate interests means that they're more likely to carry out the will of the rich and powerful than stick to the promises they made to us. What politicians *say* before an election thus ends up having only an incidental relationship with what they *do* after an election.

We are told that this is simply the nature of representative democracy. Regrettable perhaps, but unavoidable. For representation to work, representatives need a relatively free hand to deal with complex and fast-moving issues. Common citizens don't have the time or capacity to understand these issues let alone to formulate the legislation to respond to them. If citizens had the power to force representatives to do what they promised, the result would be (we are told) chaos, paralysis, and incompetence.

Of course (we are simultaneously assured), representatives shouldn't have an entirely free hand either. Some controls are obviously necessary. But these should be limited to the tried and tested methods of the pressure of public opinion and periodic elections. If politicians ignore their electorates too frequently, they can eventually be thrown out after four or five years. These mechanisms are enough (it is claimed) to ensure that representation does its job: that a group of elected rulers decide what is the common good of the people.

But just because we have been told that this is what democracy is, that doesn't mean that we have to accept it. What goes by the name of "democracy" today is in fact better thought of as "representative government," which has only a weak relationship with what was historically understood as democracy (Manin, 1997). Democracy, for many of those who fought for it, meant that representatives (or delegates) should carry out the instructions of those they represented and that there should be binding mechanisms in place to ensure this. This is known as representatives having an imperative mandate (rather than a free mandate). In what follows I'll briefly outline its history, its functioning, and its contemporary potential.

As Max Krahé argues in his essay, democracy in pre-modern political thought usually meant lotteries and not elections. By the time of the Atlantic Revolutions at the end of the eighteenth century, however, it was elections that dominated the political imaginary of revolutionaries. But there remained fierce debate over the institutional architecture surrounding elections. Who should be able to stand for election? Who should be allowed to vote? How long should terms of office be? Should voters be able to recall their representatives? And indeed, should representatives be bound by the instructions of their constituents?

The resolution of these questions took much longer than one might think. The victory of the idea that all adults should be able to vote and stand for office, without qualifications based on property, education, sex, or race, was undoubtably a huge democratic advance. But on the other institutional questions, victory went to those who explicitly opposed the advance of democracy. Elections are generally held on four- or five-year timetables rather than the annual elections proposed by radicals. Representatives are rarely subjected to the threat of being recalled and when they are it usually requires substantial hurdles. And nowhere in any constitutional democracy today are representatives held to their constituent's instructions. Indeed, many constitutions — such as those of France and Germany — explicitly ban imperative mandates for representatives.

How did we get here? An important element of the story begins in the French Revolution. When the king was forced to call a meeting of the Estates General in 1789, most of the representatives arrived with instructions from their constituents detailing how they should vote on various issues. These also often specified that the deputy should vote as part of their respective order (clergy, aristocrats, and the commoners of the so-called Third Estate). A crucial milestone in the Revolution occurred when the deputies of the Third Estate forced the other deputies to join them in a joint National Assembly without estate divisions. As part of that process the imperative mandates with which the deputies had arrived were set aside. This was initially seen as an important progressive victory over feudal institutions and the power of the clergy and the aristocracy.

But as the Revolution progressed there was growing unease amongst some radical deputies with the constitutional principle they had enshrined. Removing imperative mandates seemed to free representatives from all control by their constituents and potentially empowered a new body to oppress the people. Radicals thus turned once again to the imperative mandate as a critical element of a constitution that would establish popular power. An important success was achieved with the 1793 Jacobin constitution, which enshrined short one-year terms of office, provisions for representative recall, primary assemblies for direct political participation, popular ratification of laws, as well as allowing for imperative mandates. But the seeming victory proved short-lived as the constitution was never enacted and the reactionary turn in the Revolution buried its popular proposals.

The imperative mandate continued to feature in post-revolutionary radical thought on democracy and was defended by democrats throughout the nineteenth century, including in several Latin American countries (Colón-Ríos, 2020; Gargarella, 2013). The debate around imperative mandates came to renewed prominence in France with the Paris Commune of 1871, which briefly involved a flourishing of radical democratic ideas, including the use of imperative mandates for the deputies of the Commune (Zaidman, 2008). While the Commune was quickly suppressed, it left an important political and constitutional legacy. French radicals repeatedly attempted to implement the imperative mandate in the constitution of the

Third Republic in the 1870s and 1880s and developed a range of proposals to do so (Mollenhauer, 1998, pp. 138–66). Yet the resistance of conservatives and liberals ensured that the free mandate eventually won out. Over the following decades, the free mandate increasingly established itself as the constitutional orthodoxy in regimes that claimed to be democracies.

The radical dream of real democratic accountability was instead transferred into the idea of the political party as a mechanism to constrain the free mandate of representatives. In socialist and social-democratic thought particularly, the party was seen as the instrument through which representatives would be tied to the interests of workers. While some saw representatives' membership in the party as a sufficient guarantee of accountability, others attempted to formalize the grassroots power of party members over their representatives and developed the idea of a *party* imperative mandate. Such ideas have been a continual feature of intra-party debates and became particularly heated in the 1970s and 1980s, when radical members of the German SPD and Green Party attempted to institute imperative mandates within their parties (Kevenhörster, 1974).

The history of the imperative mandate suggests a range of institutional possibilities to realize its core idea of binding instructions for representatives. Three key questions emerge when thinking about the details of its institutionalization. (1) How extensive should instructions be? (2) What sanctions should representatives face when they fail to carry out instructions? (3) Who gives instructions and decides whether they have or have not been followed? We can summarize these as questions of *scope*, *sanctions*, and *selection*. I'll take each of these in turn.

(1) *Scope*. Opponents of the imperative mandate often assume that it implies representatives are entirely restricted to their instructions and have no freedom of action. Such a completely imperative mandate has in fact rarely been defended. Most defenders of the imperative mandate have argued that representatives are only bound when they have explicitly received instructions on a particular issue. Beyond those instructions, representatives are free to vote and act as they see fit. That might include issues that constituents have deliberately left to the representative to decide or issues unforeseen at the time of instruction. (Though defenders of the imperative mandate have also often wanted such non-instructed

issues to be subjected to subsequent controls or ratification, e.g., through popular ratification.) Additionally, instructions might also have varying levels of generality. They might simply specify the broad position that a representative should take but leave the contents of their instructions unspecified so that the representative can decide on the finer details of the issue. That would hence still allow for deliberation and compromise in legislative debates (something the imperative mandate is often accused of negating).

(2) *Sanctions.* Without sanctions for non-compliance with instructions, a supposedly imperative mandate is little more than a moral promise to uphold the wishes of constituents. Some defenders of the imperative mandate have indeed thought that the dishonor and shame that would result from breaking an election promise would be enough to ensure that representatives stuck to those promises. That has been a minority view, however, and the practice of electoral democracy suggests that representatives are more than content to weather a little shame and dishonor. Consequently, more muscular sanctions have usually been thought necessary. One simple solution is a financial sanction. That might involve a reduction of wages or the imposition of a fine on a recalcitrant representative. Such measures might also be extended to criminal charges for the representatives resulting in imprisonment. While such legal and punitive measures have featured in defenses of the imperative mandate, the principal sanctioning mechanism has been the political threat of recalling the representative. A representative who fails to carry out their instructions thus faces the possibility of being immediately removed from office. In the case of a party imperative mandate, this translates to the representative losing the whip or having their membership revoked and being unable to stand for the party at the next election. Finally, annual elections might also be thought of as a kind of sanctioning mechanism as voters have the power to sanction their representatives much more frequently than with longer terms of office.

(3) *Selection.* Probably the most important question when it comes to the realization of the imperative mandate is the perennial political question of who decides. To get a better sense of the specific options it is helpful to initially split the question of who instructs from who judges

(though as we will see the same body might carry out both tasks). One influential way of conceptualizing who instructs is to see the citizenry of each constituency as instructing their representative through the pledges made before the election. These might have a more informal character (such as the promises made by candidates in their speeches) or be formalized through meetings in which citizens compel candidates to commit to specific pledges. (That of course raises a host of further questions on the form and composition of such meetings.) Under that broad model there is then a subsequent question of who decides whether those pledges have been broken and applies the appropriate sanction. One solution defended in the debates in the French Third Republic was that the adjudicating body would be the courts and hence the judges who sit on them. On that account, the imperative mandate becomes quite similar to a legal contract, with citizens having the power to sue representatives who do not uphold their end of the contract and judges deciding whether there has been a breach of contract. That might strike many as too legal a solution and hand too much power to judges. Thus, another option considered by radicals in the Third Republic was to have committees set up at the same time as the election, which would then be responsible for judging the representative. Ideas for who might sit on such a committee included those who had nominated the candidate, local or municipal counsellors, or fellow members of the representative's party. That final option brings us closer to the idea of the party imperative mandate. The adjudicating body here was usually taken to be the constituency branch of the party. This would decide whether the representative had stuck to the pledges made to the constituency (and the wider country) in the party's election manifesto. (Under this conception, it becomes particularly salient whether the constituency branch is internally democratic.) Finally, the questions of who instructs and who adjudicates can be melded together. That is the case with the idea of primary assemblies in which each constituency has an assembly in which all of the constituency's citizens can meet to deliberate amongst themselves, and consequently instruct and sanction their representative. That idea was particularly popular during the French Revolution. It has the advantage of inclusivity but also an obvious concern with numbers.

There are thus several different ways we might realize the imperative mandate, each with advantages and disadvantages. As Rahel Süß aptly suggests in her contribution, we might take those possibilities as an invitation to experiment with different options and even combinations of options. Taking a leaf from Max Krahé's chapter on lotteries, one potential idea would be to make the body that adjudicates and sanctions the representative one that is randomly selected from the representative's constituency. Such a Constituency Assembly or Constituency Jury could perhaps be made up of 50–100 randomly selected citizens who would meet on a regular basis amongst themselves as well as with their representative. Its members would be tasked with holding the representative accountable to the constituency, by having the power to recall the representative. Since there are always unforeseen issues and changing circumstances, the representative would still have the opportunity to explain and justify to the randomly selected constituents why they diverged (or intend to diverge) from their instructions. Its members would then have the option to decide whether they found such explanations to be satisfactory. The idea of Constituency Assemblies or Constituency Juries might thus incorporate some of the popular inclusivity and control offered by Primary Assemblies (and avoid the potential elitism and exclusiveness of other solutions), while also side-stepping the worry about numbers. Lotteries might thus be one way in which the imperative mandate could be realized today.

What the imperative mandate might achieve would vary with different possible institutional realizations. One common expectation is that it would help address the appallingly limited ability of citizens to hold their representatives accountable. The current structure of our "democracies" gives representatives remarkably free reign to ignore the people they supposedly represent in the confident expectation that they will be able to ride out any outrage until the next election. In the absence of such real accountability, representatives overwhelmingly represent not their constituents but the interests of wealth and corporate power. It is these elites that currently have an imperative mandate over our representative institutions. The task before us is to ensure that it is citizens, and not these wealthy and corporate elites, that have the power to instruct our representatives.

References

Colón-Ríos, J. (2020). *Constituent Power and the Law*. Oxford University Press.

Gargarella, R. (2013). *Latin American Constitutionalism*, 1810–2010: The Engine Room of the Constitution. Oxford University Press.

Kevenhörster, P. (1974). *Das imperative Mandat: Seine Gesselschaftspolitische Bedeutung*. Herder & Herder.

Manin, B. (1997). *The Principles of Representative Government*. Cambridge University Press.

Mollenhauer, D. (1998). *Auf der Suche nach der "wahren Republik". Die französischen "radicaux" in der frühen Dritten Republik* (1870–1890). Bouvier Verlag.

Zaidman, P.-H. (2008). *Le Mandat Impératif: De la Révolution Française à la Commune de Paris*. Les Editions Libertaires.

III

SEEDS
FOR THE NEW

GENERATIVE AI AND DEMOCRACY

JUDITH SIMON

Introduction

Generative AI has taken the world by storm. This most recent summer of AI started with the launch of ChatGPT in November 2022. The usage numbers exploded and within the first two months only ChatGPT had already reached a threshold of 100 million users, a benchmark the most successful social media sites, such as TikTok and Instagram, needed considerably longer to reach.[1] In the years since, Generative AI has grown substantially with new products and services being announced with breathtaking speed. On the one hand, Generative AI is no longer confined to text but is now equally applicable to the generation of pictures as well as audio and video files, with models and tools such as Stable Diffusion, DALL-E, and Gemini already in wide usage, while others, such as the video-generator SORA, have been announced but have not yet been released at the time of writing. On the other hand, such tools are increasingly being integrated into other

---

1 By comparison, TikTok needed nine months and Instagram two years to reach the same threshold. See, for instance: https://www.theguardian.com/technology/2023/feb/02/chatgpt-100-million-users-open-ai-fastest-growing-app.

services, such as search (e.g., Bing) or office suites (e.g., Microsoft Copilot) and organizational processes in various domains. Given the failure to halt or only slow down this process through invocations of moratoria (some credible, most not), the speed of development and uptake is likely to increase rather than decrease. As a result, generative AI continues to affect a wide range of societal domains, causing upheavals in journalism and education, in science, in medicine and psychotherapy, in public administration, and in the justice system.

The core of generative AI is the capacity to produce new verbal or visual products of increasingly high quality based on patterns discovered in massive amounts of data. The difference between generative AI and earlier developments is not only improved performance, but also the fact that the tools are no longer restricted to specific domains. Due to the fundamental role of language and images for human interaction, the capacity to produce text, pictures, or videos on any topic imaginable — with high plausibility but no relation to truth — should not be underestimated: while language is the central medium of human communication, images and videos are of crucial importance for questions of evidence, for testimony, and for memory, as well as for emotions.

Apart from the high quality of output and the breadth of applicability, another important aspect that explains the unprecedented uptake of ChatGPT and other tools making use of Generative AI concerns their very high usability and availability through simple interfaces and free access via the Internet. Users need almost no previous knowledge and only low technical requirements to be able to produce and distribute texts, images, or videos of a very high quality in a matter of seconds. Prompt the systems with any request and a text or picture can be produced and amended in no time and with little effort.

These aspects explain the extremely rapid spread of ChatGPT, Dall-E, and co. — with all the positive and negative consequences associated with these AI systems. Generative AI now has many millions of regular users, billions of requests, and corresponding results, which can be used and abused for a wide variety of purposes. We therefore need to assess and combat real challenges and dangers for democracy while not being distracted by bogus debates. The latter includes, for instance, debates surrounding singularity and the end of humanity, as well as the somewhat misguided discussion about whether ChatGPT shows signs of general artificial intelligence, real understanding, or even consciousness. To be very clear: none of the current AI systems has any true understanding of the output it produces, let alone consciousness. ChatGPT detects speech patterns, the probability of word combinations, and the linguistic structure of different genres of text, based on an analysis of vast amounts of text, and it produces new texts based on these learned patterns. While one may argue that such a recognition of linguistic patterns is necessary to human understanding and that multi-modal AI systems linking text to pictures may indeed even approach a next level of "understanding", it appears farfetched to say that this is understanding in a full sense. Thus, even if ChatGPT and co. may *appear* to understand us when answering our prompts, it is worth repeating that the output generated is purely based upon the statistical analysis and reproduction of text without any true understanding of the content.

The Problems of Deception

This appearance, however, indicates one central problem of generative AI: that of deception. Indeed, Generative AI creates at least four different problems of deception.[2]

First, there are potential dangers when users wrongly believe that they are interacting with a human rather than with a machine, e.g., in contexts such as customer service or — much more problematically — in therapeutic contexts. Apart from this most obvious problem of deception, there is also the problem of deception regarding the *capabilities* of AI. Although current AI systems have neither understanding nor consciousness, it can *appear* to users that they do — even if users *know* that they are interacting with a machine. This inclination was demonstrated by early users of Weizenbaum's (1966) natural language processing software ELIZA, and is reflected in current reports on user interactions with ChatGPT. It is sometimes difficult to discern whether people truly

2   Please see Simon (2024/forthcoming) for a full-fledged analysis of the four kinds of deception caused by Generative AI.

believe that ChatGPT, Lambda, and other AI-based chatbots understand them or are conscious, or whether they are merely intentionally feeding the AI hype cycle. However, such an attribution of abilities to a machine by a human says little to nothing about the machine, but a lot about the human tendency to anthropomorphize technology. Indeed, this conflation between the *performance of "speech"* and the *ability to think* is inherent in the discourse on artificial intelligence from its inception, tracing back to the Turing Test (1950) and Searle's (1981) critique thereof.[3]

By highlighting the difference between the (nonexistent) competence of machines and the ways humans are deceived by these machines' performance, I do not aim to scoff at this human error. On the contrary, I want to issue a warning about the *performative power of simulation*: simulating intelligence, understanding, or even emotion and empathy, even if it is only a simulation, has real implications and makes us as humans vulnerable. We react cognitively and emotionally to language and images in a special way — and that is what makes these new technologies simultaneously immensely powerful and potentially harmful.

The third form of deception then concerns the deceptive results these systems generate, from funny pictures of Pope Francis in unusual clothing and videos "resurrecting" historic figures, to revenge porn, fake news, and deepfakes for propaganda purposes, from audio files "reviving" loved ones, to the criminal use of fake voices to deceive relatives. This last problem in particular poses serious challenges to societal communication and the stability of democracies. Of course, deception, propaganda, and manipulation are not new subjects. But the ease and speed with which high-quality texts, images, sound files, and videos can now be produced and distributed in real time through social media and messenger services

---

3   With the so-called Turing Test (1950), Alan Turing suggested that when a human cannot distinguish whether the responses to her queries are coming from a machine or from another human then this would be a sign of machine intelligence. John Searle countered this conclusion with his famous *Chinese room argument* (1981) in which he argued that merely successfully manipulating Chinese symbols by executing linguistic rules can and thus should be distinguished from understanding Chinese, i.e., the meaning of such symbols.

opens up a completely new dimension of possible misuse. By flooding the public sphere with false but plausible looking content, generative AI tools pose a real danger to our democracies, as fundamental processes of information and communication can be disrupted quickly, easily, and with potentially severe and lasting impacts.

The fourth and final form of deception concerns problems resulting from the integration of Generative AI into other services and products, such as web search, email programs, and office suites. Indeed, ChatGPT was initially heralded as the future of search. This misleading depiction of functions and underlying processes causes a conflation of information retrieval with information creation, which poses further challenges for evaluating information.

Taken together, these four different types of deception can cause severe epistemic, ethical, and political harm. Deception may not only cause false beliefs; the increasing difficulty of assessing the truthfulness of content may also decrease overall trust in practices and institutions of information themselves. If people feel they cannot reliably judge the quality of information nor the providers, this has potentially severe implications for public communication and democracies.

Where Do We Go from Here?

What do we do now in view of the challenges outlined above and the problems of deception in particular? In my opinion, an appropriate reaction must interweave various instruments. Neither regulation, technology design, nor education are individually sufficient, but jointly they provide our best bet to counter the challenges to democracy posed by Generative AI.

Regulation can be achieved through various forms of hard and soft law. Overall, I am rather skeptical of self-regulation in this context as industry leaders have so far not exhibited much ethical sensibility and the fear of missing out for the companies is simply too great. For that reason, we cannot rely on industry stakeholders to voluntarily commit to control their products, but rather we must ensure sound democratic control and oversight of these technologies.

In the European context, a number of laws addressing AI are already in place or are about to enter into force, such as the General Data Protection Regulation, the Digital Services Act, and the Digital Markets Act. However, the most important law in that context is the EU AI Act, which was passed in 2024. The EU AI Act, initiated before the advent of Generative AI, endorses a risk-based approach in which the regulation of AI depends on the context and sector of application. It therefore proposes specific requirements for the deployment of AI, but only in high-risk sectors or contexts, such as medicine or education. This focus on regulating critical sectors of application rather than regulating AI *tout court* has merits, but Generative AI, or so-called *general-purpose AI*, has more generally demonstrated the limits of this approach as one of its core features is precisely to be applicable *across* different sectors and domains.

So how should we regulate Generative AI then? Only when it is used in critical contexts, thereby placing the main responsibility for regulation on the deployers and professional users of Generative AI? Or do we want to place demands on the producers of Generative AI? During the AI Act Trilogue in December 2023, these questions were hotly debated within and between the European Parliament, the European Council, and the European Commission. In the end, an agreement was reached to amend the previous proposal of the AI Act and to include rules about high-impact general-purpose AI models that can cause systemic risk in the future. As the AI Act has yet to enter into force, both the interpretation of the law and its effectiveness are still open. And so is the discussion of how exactly obligations should be distributed fairly and effectively between producers, deployers, and (professional) users of such systems to respect fundamental rights and societal values.

Returning to the problem of deception, various measures for increasing transparency have been proposed. The first obvious solution concerns mandatory labeling of content provided by or with the help of AI, a requirement that is already included in the EU AI Act. Indeed, various technical solutions are currently being developed to either detect fakes or to verify true content through watermarks. Such mandatory labeling as well as technological solutions are important, but they are not sufficient to counteract the problems of deception. This labeling will not rule out criminal misuse or informational warfare. It also will not prevent people from ascribing properties to technologies that they do not have. Accordingly, there is a need to develop new norms and competencies to deal with these AI systems and to clearly identify the possibilities as well as the limitations of these systems.

More transparency can also be achieved at the level of the models themselves through open access. While ChatGPT provides free access to its basic services without fees, it is otherwise a completely proprietary and opaque system. In contrast, open-source alternatives, such as BLOOM or Stable Diffusion, allow inspecting, testing, and even modifying of the underlying technology. Such openness of course also comes with its own problems as free and open access also enables new forms of abuse. Therefore, it will be necessary to carefully examine which forms of openness have the most advantages and the fewest disadvantages. The case of ChatGPT, which combines easy and free basic access to an otherwise completely opaque and proprietary system, seems like the worst possible combination.

Finally, education is of special importance to Generative AI in at least three regards. First, it is an area that was and continues to be in itself profoundly challenged by Generative AI. Second, it is considered a high-risk area for the deployment of (Generative) AI. And third, education is central to countering the challenges Generative AI poses to democracy.

The rapid uptake of ChatGPT initially presented universities and schools with the challenge of making exams as fraud-proof as possible. The primary question revolved around how to guarantee fairness if some students have ChatGPT do their homework and others do not. More fundamentally, however, ChatGPT also opens up the possibility — and the necessity — of asking ourselves about the nature and value of education. When even students of literary studies delegate the writing of their essays to ChatGPT and texts that appear to be scientific are produced with fabricated sources, then what does this say about the goals of education and the enabling conditions at universities? Which skills and abilities still have to be learned under the condition of new technological possibilities, which ones have to be added, and which ones might no longer be needed? The German Ethics Council has provided some orientation for answering these questions in the report "Humans and Machines — Challenges Posed by Artificial Intelligence" (Deutscher Ethikrat, 2023). Our core question is how AI can be designed and used in such a way that the possibilities for human agency and authorship of the various actors involved are expanded and not reduced. It appears obvious that education on all levels and in all its different forms must encompass a solid understanding of the nature, premises, and consequences of the technological mediation of our lifeworlds. While this includes scientific, technological, and mathematical knowledge, it does not stop there. Indeed, to make use of the fruits of generative AI, but to avoid being deceived by it, this knowledge needs to be complemented with critical thinking skills, with solid knowledge, expertise and insights from the social sciences, humanities, and the arts. These knowledges crucially also need to be integrated into computer science education, to support the responsible design and development of AI technology from the onset. It is time to reassert that the foundational aim of education is not to provide learners with sellable skills and techniques, but to raise politically mature and responsible citizens. This, in the end, may be one of the biggest challenges we face if we want to secure democratic and sustainable futures.

References

Deutscher Ethikrat. (2023, March 20). *Stellungnahme Mensch und Maschine — Herausforderungen durch Künstliche Intelligenz.* https://www.ethikrat.org/fileadmin/Publikationen/Stellungnahmen/deutsch/stellungnahme-mensch-und-maschine.pdf

Searle, J. (1981). Minds, Brains, and Programs, *Behavioral and Brain Sciences*, 3, 417–57. https://doi.org/10.1017/S0140525X00005756

Simon, J. (2004/forthcoming). Generative AI, Quadruple Deception & Trust, *Social Epistemology, Special Issue: The Mind-Technology Problem: Rethinking Minds, Humans and Artefacts in the Age of AI.*

Turing, A. (1950). Computing Machinery and Intelligence. *Mind*, 59(236), 433–60. https://doi.org/10.1093/mind/LIX.236.433

Weizenbaum, J. (1966). ELIZA-A Computer Program for the Study of Natural Language Communication Between Men and Machines. *Communications of the ACM*, 9, 36–45.

EXPERIMENTAL DEMOCRACY FOR THE DIGITAL AGE

RAHEL SÜß

What is the future of democracy in the digital age? While digital technologies increasingly present challenges to democratic societies, some remain optimistic that new digital tools can help advance democracy. The central question is how can we ensure a future that is truly democratic? My proposed model of "experimental democracy" presents a new vision of democracy for the digital age. The idea is simple: the democratization of new digital technologies must go hand in hand with the democratization of society. The goal of experimental democracy is to open the future for everyone by shifting power, building sustainable communities, and promoting a political culture centered around democratic experimentation.

Today, we are living in the age of predictions. While predictive technologies are woven into the fabric of our daily lives, they increasingly threaten democratic societies. These technologies are commonly viewed as effective tools to solve various social problems. Yet, in their promise to control uncertainty and anticipate the future, they pave the way for pre-emptive strategies everywhere. Operating within such a predictability paradigm overlooks the essential fact that uncertainty is a condition of democracy. According to legal scholar Christoph Möllers (2020, p. 93, translated by the author), freedom comes to an end at the precise moment of achieving the "perfection of prevention."

More recently, predictive technologies have seen wider adoption. Judges use AI systems to advise on sentencing, and police forces employ them to predict future crimes. AI technologies are also applied in algorithmic welfare distribution systems to determine eligibility for financial support and anticipate instances of benefit fraud. Simultaneously, predictive models play a crucial role in data-driven smart city initiatives, such as the digital twin city strategy. Digital twin cities are virtual replicas of physical cities that can simulate different scenarios and test the impact of political measures, such as optimizing energy efficiency or traffic flows. Predictive technologies can also be found in generative AI systems like ChatGPT and other large language models (LLMs) that use reinforcement learning with human feedback to predict the next words in a sentence.

How dangerous are predictive technologies for democracy? Insofar as the algorithmic search for certainty and pre-emptive strategies dominate, they also raise several democratic concerns. These concerns range from closing off an open future to election fraud and beyond.

Democratic concerns include the spread of deepfakes and disinformation, as well as a tension between increasingly data-driven decision-making and democratic self-determination. Today, there are massive concerns that new digital technology will reinforce existing inequalities and enable new forms of surveillance and control. These concerns also address Silicon Valley's top-down fantasies and the increasing dependence of critical infrastructures in democratic societies on private sector players. At the same time, we face a strong centralization of power, demonstrated by monopolization tendencies from companies like Google, Microsoft, and Amazon.

Growing technocratic views pose another risk to democracy, characterized by the idea of finding a technical solution — an algorithm — for every social and political problem. While AI technologies increasingly inform political decisions, it is often unclear how these models make their predictions due to a lack of transparency in their functioning and training data. When AI technologies are used to inform decisions, there are no individuals to hold accountable. Moreover, the democratic problem extends to the data dependence of AI technologies. Concerns arise about the quality and availability of training data, given that AI systems can adopt and reproduce biases in the training data and that these systems are inherently unreliable. Given that these new technologies contribute to increased complexity, hidden risks, and social inequalities (Eubanks, 2018), the open question remains: How can we unlock the power of digital tools to strengthen democracy?

Digital democracy is often discussed as a form of *open government*. During the Obama administration, the "Transparency and Open Government" memorandum outlined guiding principles to promote transparency and collaboration between the government and its citizens (White House, 2009). Open government initiatives aim to create a more accountable, transparent, and responsive government by using new digital technologies to make government data easily accessible to the public. It is an approach to governance that aims to increase public trust in governments by creating long-term feedback loops between citizens and governments.

Digital democracy is also discussed within the context of new *experiments in participatory democracy*. The goal is to develop innovative institutional designs that foster a more participatory democratic society. An increasing number of municipalities have already used online civic engagement systems that empower citizens to influence the political agenda, suggest and prioritize reforms and legislation, and allocate municipal budgets (for an overview, see Simon et al., 2017). These participatory experiments are particularly notable for broadening our understanding of democracy beyond ideas of representative democracy. As political theorist Hélène Landemore (2021, p. 71) demonstrates, the use of digital tools allows us to move beyond a limited understanding of democratic power as mere "consent to power and delegation of power to elected elites."

Landemore's envisioned alternative (2020, 2021) is a form of non-elected democratic representation. Her work is influenced by a large-scale assembly experiment in France in which randomly selected citizens developed recommendations for climate and environmental policies. Landemore proposes a new institutional design that she calls an "open mini-public." This concept refers to a periodically renewed citizen assembly that consists of a random or stratified sample from the entire population (2021, p. 76). Digital tools play two important roles in advancing non-elected forms of democratic representation: enabling collaborative problem-solving by harnessing the collective intelligence of a large group of people and strengthening civic competence while supporting the development of new democratic cultures (ibid., pp. 77–78). Landemore also proposes the concept of a "citizenbook" as a fundamental digital infrastructure for democratic societies (ibid., p. 81). She argues that all citizens should automatically become registered members of this online platform at birth, which would then facilitate their participation in discussions and decisions. To boost engagement on these platforms, she also suggests the use of virtual chat rooms, avatars, and gamification methods (ibid., p. 73; 82).

Although there is much to recommend regarding the potential achievements of open government and participatory democracy experiments, they also give rise to various concerns. Some critics argue that citizen participation is often limited to top-down consultation exercises and mostly engages those "who are already politically active" (Simon et al., 2017, p. 83). Additional concerns include efficiency and ecological sustainability as well as a "digital divide" since "a lack of access to the internet or a lack of digital skills can be a barrier" to democratic participation (ibid., p. 88). Ultimately, it is important to note that "[d]igital technologies alone won't solve the challenges of apathy, disillusionment, low levels of trust and the widening chasm between the people and the political class" (ibid., p. 95).

To be clear, the idea that digital tools can facilitate large-scale deliberation and enhance democratic legitimacy is important, but it is not sufficient. In a context where political influence and life chances are increasingly unequal, participatory online platforms and randomly selected assemblies of citizens fall short as means of democratization. While formally including all voices in a deliberative process is an important step, it does not guarantee equal freedom, as it overlooks the structural bias in debates that favor wealthy and well-connected elites. Part of the problem is that we often understand social conflicts as conflicts of opinion rather than conflicts over resources and power. By doing so, we lose sight of the ability of political and economic elites to organize the common interest for their own benefit. This raises the question of how to boost engagement, ensure equal representation in these processes, and ensure that digital democracy can empower all citizens.

How can we use technology to enable the greatest possible participation as well as citizens' self-determination? If we understand the digital threat to democracy as originating from a predictability paradigm that risks closing off an open future, we must ask: How can a new vision of digital democracy ensure that the future remains open for everyone? I propose that experimental democracy is the way forward. Within the proposed framework, experimentation can define a future-opening practice, and political action is about experimenting. It is the freedom to experiment that characterizes a lively democracy in the digital age.

This vision of an experimental and future-opening democracy builds on radical democratic thought and pragmatist democratic experimentalism. It considers the empowering aspects of digital democracy in addition to concerns over transparency, accountability, and participation. This vision upholds values of openness and plurality while also recognizing the importance of conflict in democracy.

An experimental and future-opening democracy promotes a more radical view of democracy as a way of life. It builds on the work of the philosopher John Dewey, for whom democracy is more than just a political system or a form of government. For Dewey (1951), democracy also describes "a way of life". Political power is manifested not only in fair procedures that guarantee a minimum level of inclusion and equal influence in political decisions, but also in everyday practices, identities, relationships, and interests (Klein, 2022, pp. 31–32). Dewey's understanding of "democracy as a way of life" focuses on everyday lived experiences and the idea that citizens should have control over decisions that affect their lives.

History teaches us that democracy is not complete or static; rather, it is problematic as it has often resulted in violence and oppression. As Achille Mbembe reminds us, the history of democracy is also a history of violence and slavery (Mbembe, 2019, pp. 16–17). Today, we see continuities of historical forms of exploitation, often discussed as "digital colonialism" in the context of, for example, data labelling jobs in countries in the Global South. Empowering democracy for the digital age, therefore, must ensure that the future remains *open* for everyone.

Insofar as experimental democracy views the task of democratic societies as opening the future by negotiating alternatives, the role of conflicts becomes crucial. The key idea here is that alternative digital and democratic futures only emerge through social and political conflicts. However, it is important to understand conflicts not only as open disputes of opinion but also as conflicts over resources and power. To ensure that everyone can shape the future, we must acknowledge the historical and structurally maintained power dynamics embedded in socio-technical systems as explicated in the "Decolonizing Digital Rights" framework (Digital Freedom Fund, 2023). This framework reflects "on the way in which uneven power dynamics, exclusion, and privilege [...] shape the way in which digital rights are conceived and how they are protected" (ibid.).

Instead of viewing digital technologies as neutral tools independent of their social and political context, we need a more nuanced understanding of the interplay between technology, society, and politics. We need to ask: How are new digital technologies embedded in our society, and how do they maintain power structures? We must also explore how political decisions and economic factors have weakened communities and paved the way for new technologies to thrive. Technology affects society, and society affects our understanding, usage, and deployment of technology. This interaction can be seen, for example, through the interplay of economic incentives, political regulation, and social practices. Engaging in conflict and making conflicts visible — such as those in the supply chain (e.g., mining of precious metals, human rights violations, environmental destruction) — involves asking critical questions: Who bears the costs of digitization? How is AI developed, used, and by whom? Who benefits?

The vision of an experimental and future-opening democracy emphasizes that democracy requires not just equal opportunities for participation and influence in political decisions but also "organized collective power" (Klein, 2022, p. 27). Two ideas are particularly relevant here. Firstly, we must understand democratic institutions not only as "fair procedures for resolving disagreements", but also as mechanisms for the "organization of power in society" (ibid., p. 26; 27). Secondly, it follows from this insight that "democratic institutions [must] organize the collective power of the generally disorganized majority" (ibid., p. 39). How can experimental democracy organize collective power? Experimentation, as a practice that engages in conflict and is future-opening, can help organize collective power by opening new political imaginaries and building power.

We must ensure that technology serves democracy, the public interest, and community building. To achieve this, we need to regulate technologies and digital infrastructures in the public interest and transform data into a public good that citizens can effectively control. Community-led research, such as technology-enabled citizen science, is also a key strategy for scaling power. For example, the government in Barcelona developed a pilot program that used citizen-placed sensors to gather data on social and environmental issues, such as pollution. Based on this data, political measures to tackle the problems have been developed in a collective and participatory process.

Opening up the future for everyone also requires experimenting with power-shifting structures, such as the Workers' Algorithm Observatory (WAO). Kevin Zawacki (2023) explains that the goal of the WAO is to empower workers, including those doing gig work on Uber and other platforms, to study the black box platform algorithms. As he specifies, WAO facilitates worker-led audits where allies with specific technical skill and abilities help crowdsource and analyze data on pay, schedule, ratings, and other complex and opaque algorithmic management systems (ibid.). The WAO also serves two other empowering functions: it enables gig workers to organize for better working conditions, which allows them to rally one another and their allies to change or enforce laws and policies for their rights and protections in the platform economy (ibid.).

For an experimental and future-opening democracy to be successful, democratic practices and processes must be organized around the principle of *plurality*. Focusing on community experiences is central, as is including different stakeholders in the development of standards and rules that govern digital systems. Given that these systems shape the future of democratic societies, democratic control over them is crucial, including participating in the development of digital technologies and in decisions that influence hardware and software. Other measures include establishing decentralized structures of shared power, ensuring that citizens, workers, and communities understand the technologies that impact their daily lives, and supporting the exchange of technological skills. Ultimately, we need an ecosystem of democratic alternatives: from new ownership structures to participatory online platforms and design principles that serve communities and the environment.

When we speak of a democracy that opens up the future, it requires us to embrace *radical uncertainty* as a fundamental condition of democracy. Uncertainty is crucial because democracy demands a commitment not only to civil rights and inclusivity, but also to participatory problem-solving. The future of democracy also depends on ongoing experimentation with new political ideas and alternative practices and institutions to address today's urgent social and political challenges. A democratic culture of experimentation thrives on engaging in conflicts, acknowledging the importance of collective organizing, embracing the courage to change, and fostering a culture of failure and learning through experimentation. We need to think again in terms of social alternatives and pre-enact alternative futures. We must also create environments where individuals and social groups can experience how they can initiate change themselves. In this spirit, the future of democracy must inherently be experimental.

How does an experimental and future-opening democracy work in practice? An experimental governance model operates in three ways: by implementing a democratic experimental clause, by prototyping digital futures, and by open-sourcing democratic processes.

An experimental governance model supports, firstly, the integration of a *democratic experimental clause* into democratic procedures. The goal is to test democratic innovations and digital technologies for the public interest. As a legal instrument, the experimental clause is part of German law and provides the basis for "regulatory sandboxes" (BMWi, 2020, p. 6; BMWi, 2019, p. 7). Experimental clauses serve as a tool to test innovations, such as e-government, that cannot otherwise be tested due to existing restrictive regulations (BMWi, 2020, p. 3; 8). Crucially, an experimental governance model uses an experimental clause not only as the legal basis for regulatory sandboxes but also as a driver for democratic change. As such, it provides opportunities for developing legal, governance, and technical blueprints to strengthen new democratic politics and cultures of democratic experimentation.

This brings us to the second feature of an experimental governance model: prototyping alternative democratic and digital futures. One example of a prototype is the data governance experiment in Berlin, which aims to establish structures for data-sharing between the economy and the city of Berlin (Bielawa, 2023). Another example is The New Hanse, a data experiment by THE NEW INSTITUTE and the City of Hamburg, with the goal of developing legal, technical, and governance blueprints for data commons (The New Institute, 2023). The smart city initiative Gemeinsam Digital: Berlin provides another fascinating example for prototyping digital futures. It has developed an inclusive and participatory strategy and "a continuous learning process" for creating, testing, and developing prototypes that empower people to shape the future of the city (*Gemeinsam Digital Berlin*, 2023).

A third feature of an experimental governance model is to *open-source democratic processes*. This strategy acknowledges that the problem often lies not in open-sourcing the code but in open-sourcing the process itself. This can be achieved by establishing online libraries of successful experimental prototypes. These archives are important for effectively scaling technical, legal, and governance blueprints.

Finally, we must ask how we have succeeded in the past. The answer to this question certainly does not lie solely in technological innovations, citizens' assemblies, or discursive power. Instead, history teaches us that political movements have played a vital role in driving democratic change. To ensure a future that is truly democratic, we also need a better understanding of how pressing political issues, such as climate change, global inequalities, and new forms of oppression, are intertwined with the use of new digital technologies. Ultimately, to successfully revitalize democracy and address today's pressing challenges, democratizing AI technologies (development, access, usage, etc.) must go hand in hand with democratizing democratic societies.

References

Bielawa, H. (2023, March 30). Data Governance: Berlin startet Experiment. *Tagesspiegel Background*. https://background.tagesspiegel.de/smart-city/data-governance-berlin-startet-experiment

Bielawa, H. (2022, July 28). Hamburgs großes Datenexperiment. *Tagesspiegel Background*. https://background.tagesspiegel.de/smart-city/hamburgs-grosses-datenexperiment

Dewey, J. (1951). Democracy as a way of life. In J. Nathanson, *John Dewey: The reconstruction of the democratic life* (pp. 82–102). Charles Scribner's Sons. https://doi.org/10.1037/11125-004

Digital Freedom Fund. (2023). *Decolonizing Digital Rights in Europe*. Digital Freedom Fund. https://digitalfreedomfund.org/decolonising/

Eubanks, V. (2018). *Automating Inequality: How High-tech Tools Profile, Police, and Punish the Poor* (1st ed.). St. Martin's Press.

Federal Ministry for Economic Affairs and Energy (BMWi). (2020). *New Flexibility for Innovation. Guide for Formulating Experimentation Clauses*.

Federal Ministry for Economic Affairs and Energy (BMWi). (2019). *Making Space for Innovation. The Handbook for Regulatory Sandboxes*.

Gemeinsam Digital: Berlin. (2023). *Governance*. Berlin. https://gemeinsamdigital.berlin.de/en/strategie/governance/

Klein, S. (2022). Democracy Requires Organized Collective Power. *Journal of Political Philosophy*, *30*(1), 26–47. https://doi.org/10.1111/jopp.12249

Landemore, H. (2021). Open Democracy and Digital Technologies. In L. Bernholz, H. Landemore, and R. Reich (Eds.). *Digital Technology and Democratic Theory* (pp. 62–89). University of Chicago Press.

Landemore, H. (2020). *Open Democracy: Reinventing Popular Rule for the 21st Century*. Princeton University Press. https://doi.org/10.2307/j.ctv10crczs

Mbembe, A. (2019). *Necropolitics*. Duke University Press. https://doi.org/10.1215/9781478007227

Möllers, C. (2020). *Freiheitsgrade*. Suhrkamp.

Simon, J., Bass, T., Boelman, V., & Mulgan, G. (2017). *Digital Democracy: The Tools Transforming Political Engagement*. NESTA. http://www.nesta.org.uk/publications/digital-democracy-tools-transforming-political-engagement

THE NEW INSTITUTE. (2023). *Blueprint: Governing Urban Data for the Public Interest. A Final Report. The New Hanse Project.* https://thenew.institute/media/pages/documents/529e984d02-1698245881/the-new-hanse_blueprint_governing-urban-data-for-the-public-interest.pdf

White House. (2009). *President's Memorandum on Transparency and Open Government.* https://www.whitehouse.gov/wp-content/uploads/legacy_drupal_files/omb/memoranda/2009/m09-12.pdf

Zawacki, K. (2023). *Giving Gig Workers the Transparency They Deserve.* Mozilla Foundation. https://foundation.mozilla.org/en/blog/giving-gig-workers-the-transparency-they-deserve/

PLANETARY DEMOCRACY: TOWARDS RADICAL INCLUSIVITY

FREDERIC HANUSCH

I. The Need for Planetary Democracy

The planet must be taken into account when democracy is defined, practiced, and evaluated. Democracies interact with planetary forces, from (induced) seismicity to (anthropogenic) space weather, and are often mediated by technologies ranging from hardware sensors to machine learning algorithms. Pandemics, extreme weather, or forest fires fostered by human activity increasingly shift democratic practice from action to reaction. We do not simply live on a planet, we are a part of it. Our democracies, however, do not reflect this.

Taking Abraham Lincoln's famous definition of democracy in the Gettysburg Address (1863) as a *government of, by and for the people* as a starting point, one only has to add three words to this definition to move democracy towards radical inclusivity: *and the planet*.

What does that mean? In the case of the oldest existing nation-state democracy, when Lincoln formulated this definition, "the people" meant white male property owners. It was only in 1920 that the 19th Amendment to the US Constitution granted women the right to vote, and it took until 1965 for the Voting Rights Act to do away with discriminatory practices that had kept Black people from voting. Each stage of inclusion, which has taken place in similar but different forms around the globe, contributed to a democratization of democracies. When those who had lacked agency and were seen primarily as a resource for labor or reproduction were included, they reshaped democracies and redistributed power, and, as a result, opened up new opportunities for a better quality of life for many.

It is not just the exclusion of various humans that is a democratic failure — so too might be the exclusion of non-humans. A simple change of words can reveal this. Sir James Grant, member of parliament for Whitehaven, spoke on May 5, 1913 in the Parliament of the United Kingdom:

> "[M]en have the vote and the power at the present moment; I say for Heaven's sake let us keep it. We are controlled and worried enough by women at the present time, and I have heard no reason given why we should alter the present state of affairs." (Grant, 1913)

Throughout the history of democracy, it is easy to find similar views about marginalized groups, ranging from children to migrants to people with disabilities. To illustrate the purpose of radical inclusivity towards the planet advocated for in this intervention, one can change two words of the statement above:

> "Humans *have the vote and the power at the present moment; I say for Heaven's sake let us keep it. We are controlled and worried enough by the* planet *at the present time, and I have heard no reason given why we should alter the present state of affairs."*

If we do not invent novel forms of democracy that include the more-than-human, then anthropocentric, epistemic, and thus political oppression will prevail. A truly planetary account of democracy is therefore a radically inclusive one that keeps the Earth habitable. It has to extend towards the inclusion of (in)active matter, flora and fauna, and artificial intelligence. Thus, it must combine the "all-affected principle", i.e., all those affected by a decision should be involved in its making, with an "all-effect principle" that encompasses all the planetary agencies that effect democracies.

II. Establishing Planetary Democracy

A planetary democracy has to take the more-than-human world into account by recognizing the interconnectedness of humans and non-humans. For example, in New Zealand, Mount Taranaki, the Whanganui River, and the Te Urewera rainforest have all recently become legal entities with spokespersons representing their interests, an initiative that was initiated by the indigenous Māori (Geddis and Ruru, 2020). Such environmental personhood also exists for the Ganges River in India, which has its own "right to life," for part of the Amazon rainforest, which was declared a legal person in Columbia, and for the saltwater lagoon Mar Menor in Spain. Ecuador has even enshrined the "Rights of Nature" in its constitution, as an inalienable right of ecosystems to exist and flourish. Similar to designating environmental personhood, the European Parliament convened a Commission to investigate the possibility of conferring electronic personhood on autonomous robots that "make autonomous decisions or otherwise interact with third parties independently" (European Parliament, 2017).

However, a planetary democracy goes beyond the realization of non-human personhood through human proxy representation. Here, the "by" in Lincoln's Gettysburg definition is not realized since the non-human does not itself participate. The same holds true for academic and artistic proposals to represent non-humans. To take the "by" seriously in such proposals, micro-level interpretations of the possibly political activities non-humans engage in are required — but this calls for listening practices that exceed the capabilities of human senses (Mejer, 2019). This can be achieved, however, through the potential of sensors, machine learning, and semiotics that allow humans to understand, for example, communication between bats that is otherwise indecipherable to human ears, or electronic impulses sent by mycological organisms that are thought to be comparable to human language (Adamatzky, 2022; Chaverri et al., 2018; Romero et al., 2021).

The precondition to take the "by" seriously and to directly include the non-human is likely to be met within the next few years as our knowledge of non-human communication and collective decision-making increases.

Sperm whales, for example, are a species with advanced brain structures, mental skills, group behaviors, and distinct clicking sounds for communication. The Cetacean Translation Initiative (CETI, www.projectceti.org) uses robots to capture large amounts of these sounds, which machine learning algorithms analyze to identify sperm whale communication patterns and, potentially, to one day be able to communicate with them (Andreas et al., 2022). Researchers are not only conducting comparable studies on the consciousness and communicative systems of other non-human animals — such as the naked mole-rat (Barker, 2021) — they are also examining the means through which flora communicate via the Mycorrhizal networks of forests, or the ways in which (in)active matter arranges itself in and through volcanos (Calvo et al., 2021; Simard, 2021). What is more, it is becoming apparent that non-human life forms engage in interspecies dialogue with each other. Plants can perceive and discern the sounds of specific insects, which allows them to tell the harmful from the harmless; for instance, flower heads fill their nectaries within minutes if bees fly into their proximity. The world echoes with the planet's sounds, which human ears cannot hear — but technologies can (Bakker, 2022). Additionally, collective decision-making does not rely only on features mostly ascribed to neurotypical humans. Large groups of red deer rest while chewing their food, and the herd decides to leave a resting place when more than half of the adults have gotten up; they use their legs to signal their choice. Many other species use their bodies to drive collective decision-making processes forward, including buffalos, pigeons, and honeybees (Bridle, 2022).

Even more, new technologies can be used, from inner Earth to interplanetary space, to identify signs and meanings of vast more-than-human agencies across Earth's spheres, such as hurricanes. It might not always be possible to communicate with these entities, yet it is feasible to establish functional relationships with (in)active matter, such as magnetism and gravity, or the phenomenon of vibration. Take gravitation's agency, ranging from effects on our bodies to our settlements as an example. Recent theories even suggest that human bodies may grow hypersensitive to gravitational forces due to stress factors, such as weight gain or irregular sleeping patterns, with potential impacts on their gastrointestinal health (Wapner,

2023). In addition to affecting human bodies, the moon's gravitational pull causes oceanic waters to shift in tidal patterns, which has shaped human societies and their settlements significantly and continues to do so (Coughenour et al., 2009). These planetary forces are barely present in today's politics and are not up for compromises or common agreements, but rather act in the form of cause–effect. Similarly, the exchange with artificial intelligence, as it is applied in seemingly autonomous robots and in the wider technosphere, effects democracies, thereby necessitating careful consideration of direct participation in a planetary democracy.

The establishment of planetary democracy will require extensive democratic experimentation, the likes of which are demonstrated by pioneering initiatives, such as the Embassy of the North Sea (www.embassyofthenorthsea.com) or the Terrao forest that owns itself (https://terrao.org). We must identify which institutions — and not necessarily those centered around a parliament — and which processes, designed to also include non-humans unable to communicate verbally, need to be invented. Therefore, humans should enter into exchange with (in)active matter, flora and fauna, and artificial intelligence. We must also analyze whether, for the integrity of ecoregions, bioregions, and biogeographic realms, their collective yet differentiated "will" can be identified, as is already done with the aggregation of political will at the level of states, countries, or supranational organizations that might be reconfigured based on Anthromes. Experimentation in this direction can use the insights gathered from, for example, the Destination Earth (DestinE) initiative of the European Union, which aims to build a digital twin of the Earth to observe, model, and forecast the interplay between natural events and human activities.

Despite the acknowledgement of non-human agency, a planetary democracy has to retain human responsibility. Humans control the inclusion and exclusion of knowledges and ways of being: even a more-than-human political institution and respective processes would have to be established by humans. Accordingly, potential barriers to a planetary democracy have to be considered, including anthropocentric path dependencies on mental, institutional, and material infrastructures. During the period of experimentation with planetary approaches to democracy, uncertain situations with multiple and diverse forms of more-than-human agencies are likely to pose challenges. In particular, humans might fear being equated with the non-human and losing control over the planet — a control we never actually had.

III. Possible Implications of Planetary Democracy

The realization of a planetary democracy can have at least three effects. First, a planetary democracy can democratize democracies, enabling recognition of their proactive agency in shaping the future. It is hardly surprising that, to date, democracies barely recognize the bi-directionality of planet–human relations. When the constitutions of most Western democracies were written, the Enlightenment paradigm painted a picture of society being freed from earthly rhythms and the chains of nature. This supposed de-coupling from nature ultimately became a planet-wide problem, as humans have massively expanded their influence on the Earth's systems since the Great Acceleration, namely the simultaneous rise of socioeconomic human activity and its impact on the Earth's systems (Steffen et al., 2015). During the Anthropocene, human societies have acquired planetary forces, and creative leeway to change the planet has emerged, yet institutions that might democratize this leeway have been and still are missing. As a consequence, democracies are now being confronted not only with various planetary feedbacks, such as wildfires, but also with movements whose claims range from regressive "Great-Again" "retrotopias" of a romanticized fossil fuel-based past to technocratic calls for a climate emergency (vvv and Meisch, 2022). A planetary democracy aims to capture and democratize creative leeway, thus eroding the basis for these movements. Avenues towards a planetary democracy begin to form, for example, when movements propagate an intersectional environmentalism in which the struggle for civil rights and the struggle for the planet converge (www.intersectionalenvironmentalist.com).

Second, a planetary democracy is more likely to ensure that this planet remains habitable. A planetary account of democracy can reconnect societies with the planet and advance the recognition of their interdependence and responsibility towards the more-than-human. It thus fosters respect for the diversity and integrity of (in)active matter, flora and fauna and, most recently, a technosphere. This approach of keeping the planet habitable in a radically inclusive manner, grounded in an understanding of the interconnectedness of all beings and elements within the larger cosmos, has been identified as "cosmovivialism": "[C]osmovivir may be a proposal for a partially connected commons achieved without canceling out the uncommonalities among worlds because the latter are the condition of possibility of the for¬mer: a commons across worlds whose interest in common is uncommon to each other" (de la Cadena, 2015, pp. 285–86).

Third, a planetary account of democracy can help to leave behind (inter)nationalism by including the non-human in world politics (Pereira et al., 2020; Pedersen, 2020). Nation-states and the international system are not natural or fixed entities. They are historical and contingent constructions that have only emerged as the dominant political order within the last centuries — and not all countries are nation-states and some nations have no state. By creating novel political planetary entities, such as ecoregions, bioregions, and biogeographic realms, in addition to or even as a long-term replacement for nation-states, democracies can emerge in line with the earthly multitudes necessary to cope with and flourish within the multiplicity of an ever-changing planet (Clark and Szerszynski, 2020). To "think like a planet" is thus also an act of freeing humankind from the chains of an anthropocentric and nation-state centered world view.

Just as planetary scientists propose formulas approximating the state of the universe, social scientists and humanities scholars must propose and justify institutions that approximate the state of societies within this universe as part of planet Earth. The time to do so is now.

References

Adamatzky, A. (2022). Language of Fungi Derived from Their Electrical Spiking Activity. *Royal Society Open Science*, 9(4). https://doi.org/10.1098/rsos.211926

Andreas, J., et al. (2022). Toward Understanding the Communication in Sperm Whales. *Iscience*, 25(6). https://doi.org/10.1016/j.isci.2022.104393

Bakker, K. (2022). *The Sounds of Life: How Digital Technology is Bringing Us Closer to the Worlds of Animals and Plants*. Princeton University Press.

Barker, A. J., et al. (2021). Cultural Transmission of Vocal Dialect in the Naked Mole-rat. *Science*, 371, 503–507. https://doi.org/10.1126/science.abc6588

Bridle, J. (2022). *Ways of Being: Beyond Human Intelligence*. Penguin.

Calvo, P., Baluška, F., & Trewavas, A. (2021). Integrated Information as a Possible Basis for Plant Consciousness. *Biochemical and Biophysical Research Communications*, 564, 158–165. https://doi.org/10.1016/j.bbrc.2020.10.022

Chaverri, G., Ancillotto, L., & Russo, D. (2018). Social Communication in Bats. *Biological Reviews*, 93(4), 1938–1954. https://doi.org/10.1111/brv.12427

Clark, N., & Szerszynski, B. (2020). *Planetary Social Thought: The Anthropocene Challenge to the Social Sciences*. John Wiley.

Coughenour, C. L., Archer, A. W., & Lacovara, K. J. (2009). Tides, tidalites, and secular changes in the Earth–Moon system. *Earth-Science Reviews*, 97(1–4), 59–79. https://doi.org/10.1016/j.earscirev.2009.09.002

de la Cadena, M. (2015). *Earth Beings: Ecologies of Practice Across Andean Worlds*. Duke University Press. https://doi.org/10.2307/j.ctv11smtkx

European Parliament. (2017). *Resolution on Addressing Refugee and Migrant Movements: The Role of EU External Action* (2015/2342(INI)). https://www.europarl.europa.eu/doceo/document/TA-8-2017-0051_EN.html

Geddis, A., & Ruru, J. (2019). Places as Persons: Creating a New Framework for Māori-Crown Relations. In J. Varuhas & S. W. Stark (Eds.), *The Frontiers of Public Law*. Hart Publishing.

Grant, J. (1913). Representation of the People (Women) Bill. https://api.parliament.uk/historic-hansard/commons/1913/may/05/representation-of-the-people-women-bill

Hanusch, F., & Meisch, S. (2022). The Temporal Cleavage: The Case of Populist Retrotopia vs. Climate Emergency. *Environmental Politics*, 31(5), 883–903. https://doi.org/10.1080/09644016.2022.2044691

Lincoln, A. (1863). Gettysburg Address "Nicolay copy." http://www.loc.gov/exhibits/gettysburg-address/ext/trans-nicolay-copy.html

Meijer, E. (2019). *When Animals Speak: Toward an Interspecies Democracy* (vol. 1). NYU Press.

Pedersen, S. (2020). Planetarism: A Paradigmatic Alternative to Internationalism. *Globalizations*. 18(2), 141–154. https://doi.org/10.1080/14747731.2020.1741901

Pereira, J. C., & Saramago, A. (Eds.). (2020). *Non-Human Nature in World Politics: Theory and Practice*. Springer.

Simard, S. (2021). *Finding the Mother Tree: Uncovering the Wisdom and Intelligence of the Forest*. Penguin.

Steffen, W., Broadgate, W., Deutsch, L., Gaffney, O., & Ludwig, C. (2015). The Trajectory of the Anthropocene: The Great Acceleration. *The Anthropocene Review*, 2(1), 81–98. https://doi.org/10.1177/205301961456478

Wapner, J. (2023, March 15). The Rogue Theory That Gravity Causes IBS. *The Atlantic*. https://www.theatlantic.com/health/archive/2023/03/gravity-cause-disease-irritable-bowel-syndrome-theory/673407/

INCORPORATING FUTURES INTO DEMOCRACY: IMAGINING MORE

MAKI SATO

The modernization of science has enabled us to look into the future using numerical figures and computer modeling. Today, models are intensively used for future predictions in our daily lives. From short-term local weather forecasts to longer-term climate change, economic growth, how you age, etcetera, etcetera, today almost everything can be predicted through modeling. With sufficient past data and a simplified representation of reality as key parameters, models provide us with a probable future, and we make decisions based on that probable future predicted by models. In short, we make decisions by forecasting our future using computer models. In that sense, we create what we perceive of the natural world in the digital world. There is nothing new about digital twins; we have gone way beyond making digital twins, and society depends on predictions for the future by models that affect our decision-making. However, these predictions are based on the limited imaginations and creative ideas of scientists and academics who rely on past numerical facts and Bayesian probability. This approach, akin to gazing into a crystal ball, is simply an extension of the past and the present. I propose that the future is much more. It can be open and inviting to every human co-becoming[1] and all stakeholders in the future of democracy through humanity's gifted ability to be creative and imaginative. Democracy of the future should not allow the voiceless voices of the future or silenced voices of non-humans to be ignored; instead, it should try to incorporate them into the decision-making process. It's crucial that we value and include diverse voices in our vision of the future of democracy, as their perspectives and experiences are integral to shaping a future that is truly representative and just. Inclusivity in decision-making is not just a concept but a practice that values and respects the contributions of all individuals in the democratic process.

In the Japanese science fiction novel *Harmony* (2010) by Project Itoh, Miaha tells her friend Tuan with a sigh, "The future is in one-word 'boredom,' *we are trapped in a dungeon called future envisioned by the old people.*"[2] How can we prevent future generations from feeling like Miaha and prevent creating a future based on the past? I know that if we are to limit ourselves to picturing our future through our present experiences, we will fail members of future generations. How could our grandparents have known and predicted that half of our days would be spent using digital devices? Models prepared by our grandparents could not have predicted our lifestyle today.

We all know that we need a drastic change in our deadlocked society. Some say capitalism and some say left-wing liberals or right-wing nationalists are to blame. Yet, we don't know precisely what will trigger the change because of the interdependent networks of systemic complexity. In other words, even if we are to solve one problem, no one knows how that solution may create a new type of problem. However, I see that the future we want for our descendants is not what scientists predict, which is often sadly linked with the idea of doomsday. In order to get past our deadlocked situation, we must be motivated to upgrade the system of representative

1   Human co-becoming implies the notion of dynamic mutuality between human beings, which suggests that humans can only become more human through interaction and inter-relationality. Just as babies cannot survive independently without parental care, humans are inherently interdependent and can survive and grow from mutual interactions.

2   Italicization has been added by the author.

democracy. This upgrade will not only welcome stakeholders of a new imagined community but will also unite us based on our shared common future, thereby fostering a sense of commitment and dedication to the proposed changes. This vision of a united, committed future should inspire hope and optimism in all of us. Why is the intervention that serves future generations within the system of democracy crucial? The twin global environmental problems of climate change and biodiversity loss exhort humans to work together toward the justifiable and hopefully egalitarian use of the social common goods. Inge Kaul defines global commons as "(goods) having nonexcludable nonrival benefits that cut across borders, generations, and populations" (Kaul et al., 2003). This definition of global commons implies that, in our decision-making process, we urgently need to combine the perspective of global commons and a shared common future with a longer perspective. Democratic decisions thus need to become more future-inclusive and consider the distant future of 30–50 years from now. In that sense, fiscal year planning or thinking 3–5 years ahead is not sufficient. We must allow ourselves to have a longer-term perspective in planning our shared future and should include the imagined shared futures in our current democratic system.[3]

Whether we like it or not, we, the citizens of the earth, are reminded every day that we are compelled to be involved in a grand social experiment on Spaceship Earth. The concept of *Spaceship Earth* proposed by Buckminster Fuller in 1968 has never been more keenly felt than now because of the climate catastrophe and severe bio-diversity loss we face.[4] But we shouldn't worry: the future has always been, and will always be, chaotic. The essential question is how we redesign, adjust, and prepare our

3   In Wales, the Well-being of Future Generations (Wales) Act 2015 endows the Future Generations Commissioner for Wales with a unique role. The Commissioner acts as the guardian of future generations and helps public bodies and policymakers in Wales consider the long-term impact of their decisions. See https://www.futuregenerations.wales/ for more details.

4   The Spaceship Earth metaphor is a powerful tool that helps people understand the finite nature of our planet and the need for humans to operate within its limits. It underscores the interconnectedness of human actions and the necessity for collective action to prevent human-caused catastrophes.

society for that chaotic future. Computer modeling simulations based on cause-and-effect trajectories may identify some possible future aspects. The problem is not the scientific accuracy of these predictions. Instead, it is how we, the current generation, prepare for the future as we deepen our understanding of the root causes of the problems and how we design the ideal future to include future generations. We forecast the near future and plan accordingly. At least, this is how the current democracy generally works, based on what I call the *forecast model of democracy*.[5] But I have a counter-proposal to the current model, a proposal I call a *backcast model of democracy*, which starts by using our ability to imagine and create an ideal distant future for our shared future society and works back from there.

The ideal conceptual future democracy would be equally inclusive of all living and non-living beings on our planet, viewing each one as a member of a planetary citizenry. Philosophers like Bruno Latour have hinted at the importance of inviting others who coexist with us on Earth, including non-humans, into the "Parliament of Things." Although there is no direct link to what Latour proposed, in 2017, a robot named Sophia was given legal personhood in Saudi Arabia. The Whanganui River in New Zealand was granted the same legal rights as humans in the same year. These incidents do not explicitly imply whether non-living or non-human beings are included in the system of democracy, especially when we are still struggling to extend equality to all human races and genders. However, one apparent thing is that democracy has always been and continues to be about expanding its *horizontal* democratic sphere. This expansion has gone from inviting non-aristocratic men to participate (the etymology of democracy is from the ancient Greek words *demos* [δῆμος], the ordinary people, and *kratos* [κράτος], power, so the power of the people), to eventually including women, and gradually to the possibility of inviting other living and non-living things to be stakeholders in the democratic system.

So, how can we incorporate the silenced members of our society, future generations, and non-human and non-living beings into our democracy? The *present generation* is the connection point between people who

5   As argued above, the forecast model of democracy incorporates model prediction into its decision-making process. However, such prediction is based on a simplified understanding of the natural world, using past data as its prediction base.

lived in a distant past that no longer exists and people who will live in a distant future that does not exist yet. In other words, the present generation represents a bridge between past and future generations and is entrusted with decision-making regarding the different stakeholders. So, shouldn't the present generation act on behalf of the speechless voices of earthly human co-becomings in the representative system of democracy, inclusive of future generations of non-humankind?[6] In the ideal future democracy, a playful role-play in the "Parliament of Things" should be realized that allows representative members to speak for the silent voices of future generations, trees, plants, animals, and non-living things, such as rivers, mountains, seas, robots, and, perhaps, AI. Future democracy must be about loosening and opening the human *ability for creativity* and the *capacity of imagination* to create a more diverse and inclusive congress. This is also crucial to the backcast method of democracy I introduced above. We first have to imagine our ideal shared *distant future*. In other words, the backcast method is a way to fill in the gaps of the imagined shared future and work backward to create that imagined future from the present, trying to fill in the gaps from now to make that ideal imagined future. In short, it is the opposite of what we are doing today through model-based decision-making, which forecasts from the present to predict the future. However, the future remains uncertain because of the lack of a shared view of an ideal future. The backcast method of democracy attempts to incorporate our shared view of an ideal future into the decision-making process. My dear reader, what would you like to see in our ideal possible future?

How should we proceed to apply intergenerational democracy based on the imagined community? One perspective of embracing human co-becoming stresses the importance of realizing mutuality, connectivity, and reciprocity for humans to become more human, which is the concept of human co-becoming. When facing the problem of a planet that is filled with future uncertainties, it becomes crucial to look beyond the *horizontal*

---

6   I propose inviting non-human and non-living beings into the democracy as members of the Parliament of Things. Referring to the metaphor of Spaceship Earth reminds humans that we need not only humans, which is already quite a dominant species, to become human co-becomings. But non-humans and non-living beings of the earth should count as members of the Spaceship Earth, as should the crucial agencies and entities that help us humans grow to become better beings.

nature of the democratic sphere and address the *vertical* realm of the democratic sphere that invites future generations of humans, as well as human co-becomings, to be part of the distant future. In recent years, several European countries, including Austria, Belgium, and Germany, have lowered the voting age to teenagers aged sixteen and over to incorporate the voices of the (near) future. However, many adults are further concerned with lowering the voting age out of fear of putting too much responsibility on children. In short, the current limited (or rational) thinking fails to invite "others," both human and non-human, who will be part of our distant future to add their as-yet-unheard voices to the social democratic system.

So, how can we listen to and incorporate the voices of future generations (and non-humans)? I think the key is expanding the current generation's imagination and creativity and looking deeper into the current society. In whatever attempts we make, we are permanently gridlocked in the present in a certain forever-*presentness*, and we can only think about the future from where we are now: from *here and now*.[7] Therefore, I propose that our imagined community — and I'm partially borrowing this idea of an "imagined community" from Benedict Anderson's touchstone book on nationalism — should extend its notion in terms of timescale. Simply put, Anderson's argument identifies the elements for the rise of nationalism as religious communities, printing industries, and the use of language, which is far different from the current rise of the right-wing nationalist movements. Suppose nationalism is the sense of belonging to the nation-state. In that case, I propose that if we had a shared *global* history beyond mere state histories, the sense of belonging to a shared planetary community could develop a new type of imagined community that allows us to envision our common Imagined Future and bring it into being.

But how can we stretch our imagination and creativity given the issue of "presentness"? The illusion of modernity suggests that we can determine what is right by understanding events through the verifiability of science via quantification, digitization, and computer modeling. In other words, modern science has successfully pushed the *belief system* toward numbers

---

[7] Yes, right! This is inspired from Zen Buddhist thought. Zen is not only about meditation and mindfulness – action from here and now is constantly required.

and quantification, away from the mystique religious belief system. Using this logic, a distant future will require us to maximize our trust in the human ability to imagine and play, away from blind faith in numbers and quantity. For example, through GNP, we can predict economic status using numbers. However, GNP growth does not necessarily imply that we will find happiness and satisfaction in our future life. A future democracy calls for a design based on *qualitative* aspects, not *quantitative* ones — not merely an extension of the past and the present to the predictable future, but a playful imagination of the ideal future beyond cause and effect. The future is filled with uncertainty. Thus, I propose that now is the time to maximize humanity's playfulness, imagination, and creativity to make humans more humane through mutuality and reciprocity beyond the predicted deadlocked future anticipated by computer models. Instead of being fearful and saddened by a future predicted by computer modeling or AI, we need to dream together the shared ideal common future, the imagined Shangri-la, and then backcast from that ideal state to identify what are the feasible steps that we can take now to make our society better.

By producing a new perspective to realign existing issues, such as how to govern the global commons more justly beyond nationalism and national borders, we can design a different path for the possible future. If we continue on the present path with limited imagination and chain ourselves to the finiteness of the data we can obtain, the possibility of our shared future will be reduced. In other words, we can only design an ideal future if it is not based on the predictions of quantitative analysis but rather if the present generation seriously considers the future we want with playful thoughts. As citizens sharing the vision of an ideal collaborative Shangri-la future, we invite the future generation, including non-human and non-living beings, into the imagined community that ties us with the notion of a shared future. Is this radical? I don't think so. We had already opened our doors to the imagined community that shares our common future when the Club of Rome first published *The Limits to Growth* in 1972, which links the potential for a future to choices made today. However, the problem with that attempt and subsequent attempts to consider the future have been based on computer modeling that relies on quantitative analysis. Making democratic policy decisions with the distant future in mind has been ongoing for quite a while, especially since we became aware of the harm we are inflicting on our planet and how that impacts our shared future.[8] Still, we have been bound by conventions. We are limited to always thinking and navigating with fear that confronts us with risks, dangers, and hazards of what might happen, thereby restricting our minds from dreaming freely. We must take a deep breath and believe our distant future can be bright, happy, and backcast from that shared ideal future to change how we think, imagine, and dream, starting today.

As a tentative conclusion, I would like to summarize what this idea could achieve. Using imagination, we can envision ourselves as a tree cut down in the rainforest, a contaminated, smelly, and polluted river, or an oxidated sea where sea mammals and fish suffocate. We could also imagine ourselves as a time traveler representing future generations, returning from the distant future to advise the current generation on what could be done *now* to change the conventional path — my proposed backcast method. We need to remind ourselves of our ability to dream playfully about our shared future and how we want our society to be in the next 30 to 50 years. Through such a thought exercise, we can incorporate the ideal virtual future, our dream society, into our democratic system. How do we want our society to be when our children and grandchildren are grown? It is up to the present generation to decide whether we will be flexible and comfortable with our imagination and creativity. By incorporating this imagined common future now, we can open the different and alternating possibilities of intergenerational democracy based on our shared ideal future.

[8] The United Nations is currently drafting the United Nations Declaration on Future Generations aimed at the Summit of the Future, which is to be held in September 2024. The idea behind this declaration is to consider the interests of future generations in national and global decision-making. For more details, refer to https://www.un.org/en/summit-of-the-future/declaration-on-future-generations.

References

Anderson, B. R. O. (1983). *Imagined Communities: Reflections on the Origin and Spread of Nationalism*. Verso.

Fuller, R. B. (1978). *Operating Manual for Spaceship Earth*. E.P. Dutton.

Kaul, I. (Ed.). (2003). *Providing Global Public Goods: Managing Globalization*. Oxford University Press. https://doi.org/10.1093/0195157400.001.0001

Latour, B., & Porter, C. (2004). *Politics of Nature: How to Bring the Sciences into Democracy* (C. Porter, Trans.). Harvard University Press.

Meadows, D. H., Meadows, D. L., Randers, J., & Behrens, W. (1972). *The Limits to Growth: A Report for the Club of Rome's Project on the Predicament of Mankind*. Universe Books.

Project Itoh. (2010). *Harmony* (A. O. Smith, Trans.). Haikasoru.

Sato, M. (佐藤, 麻貴). (2022). 未来社会2050−学問を問う(Future Society 2050 — The Role of Academics). In East Asian Academy, The University of Tokyo et al. (Eds.) 私たちは世界の「悪」にどう立ち向かうか (*How are We to Confront Evils of the World*), (pp.263–302). Transview.

Sato, M. (佐藤, 麻貴). (2021).円環と直線の交点−わたしたちは現在をどう引き受けるのか(The Intersection of Circles and Lines: How Do We Take on the Present?). In T. Saijo. et al. (Eds.) フューチャー・デザインと哲学　世代を超えた対話 (*Future Design and Philosophy: Intergenerational Dialogue*), (pp.69–97). Keiso.

AN ART OF ASSOCIATION: DEMOCRACY AND DANCE

ANNA KATSMAN

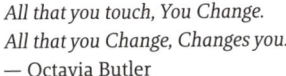

> *All that you touch, You Change.*
> *All that you Change, Changes you.*
> — Octavia Butler
>
> *Could it be that pausing, sensing and playful lightness*
> *are not tools on the way to a new story,*
> *but that they are the new story?*
> — Heike Pourian

You enter a room and find others spread out generously around the space, some standing, some laying down, some moving, some still. To enter is also to arrive. To arrive is to ask yourself what you need in order to be there, to be present, to be available to yourself and only therewith to the others with whom you will share the experience to come. This practice is called Contact Improvisation; it can be made available in the everyday life of civil society, is self-organized by the people committed to it, open to anyone interested, and offers direct, personal experience of experimenting with and intimately embodying democratic life. For there is more to democracy than voting for representatives, political campaigns, parliamentary meetings, creating and enforcing laws, judicial hearings, and the rights and responsibilities of national citizenship. These structures are themselves based on a set of norms, values, and commitments that inform a way of associating.

You begin by opening your perception, sensing yourself, sensing others, sensing the interfaces between self and other. You begin to notice the many feelings you hold, consciously and subconsciously, which you repress in daily life, but which nevertheless subtly create the mood that frames your perception: accumulated tension, or maybe excitement;

inspiration or fatigue; tentativeness or curiosity; amusement or unnoticed aggression, whatever it may be. Your first work is to make honest contact with yourself, for you are about to enter into sensitive connection with others where what is at stake is not showing up as a rational, well-functioning, well-disciplined individual who has mastered the relevant social scripts, but rather honestly exploring what it means to show up and connect with others in light of how you actually feel within the parameters of interpersonal respect.

You begin to move on the basis of your impulses and wonder where they come from. Are they your own? Do they stem from others in the room, whether through mimesis or an effort to impress? Where do you seek inspiration? Do you have the courage to try another way? Others move around you on the basis of their impulses. You sense agency in their movements as you sense your own ability to move. You feel the freedom each individual gives the others while simultaneously articulating an atmosphere together, allowing flutters of mutual inspiration; momentarily echoing and being echoed in turn.

At what point does dancing separately together become dancing together, cueing one another's movements, recognizing another's impulse as an occasion for one's own, and being thereby opened to new possibilities for your own movement, freedom enhanced and enabled in and through another? This is a question of sensing — mutual sensing. Is the other open to dancing with you as the possibilities of togetherness evolve out of this moment? Are you?

Arriving with one another, finding the tempo of that arrival, both feel for cues for an invitation to mutuality. A point of contact, touch, emerges between us and we lean in softly, discovering and calibrating who we are in our encounter. How do we find equal weight together to engender a stable structure around which we are able to move? Do you trust me to take your weight — or what would it take for you to begin to trust me? Exploring, we learn that when we both release our weight into one another — and it turns out we have to give more than we anticipated! — we can release ourselves into the structure we also uphold.

Working from points of contact, our aim is neither to lead nor to follow, but to allow our mutual movement to guide us together. You pivot your side around my torso, your leg finds space, and you suspend in float for a moment. Experimenting, we begin to loosen the hard distinction between creation and discovery, dependence and independence. The impulse we share links our agency and together with you I have new possibilities of expressive movement. In so doing, we overcome our isolation and nourish a shared sense of the world. We tap into human social creativity and establish the conditions that empower us to be active agents, individually and collectively creating our own trajectories. You offer me a shoulder on which to climb and now I balance. The pleasures of free self-expression here are not located in an empty room that I take for myself alone, but in the inspiration for new possibilities of expression you make room for and evoke in me.

The effort of communication through physical contact requires and cultivates a sensibility of mutual listening, trust building, learning how to co-decide and co-create, and being cared for in vulnerable fleshiness. Your head falls onto my shoulders and I softly guide you to the floor, tumbling down with you. My torso enables your vulnerability, your trust, and your joy in having the support to fall, release your uprightness, and find the floor on which to rest and take momentary refuge. We land and pause, sighing with our bodies, leaning on one another, listening for the needs of time and cues to begin again. We reverse course. I now pour into the structure you construct around me. Release is known by having held; holding is known by having released. We are conducting personal research into the forces of gravity to which we are subject both actively and passively, but with an ethical aim — how do we bring ease and lightness into our collective work with the material forces on which we depend, and which shape us? How do we teach and learn from one another in so doing? In a culture of increasing privatization, digitalization, and materialistic consumption as a way of life, we are fostering a commitment to togetherness by building up the sensibilities of solidarity and trust with each other, a solidarity and trust itself based on strengthening our ability to listen to and hear one another, be vulnerable with one another, and be cared for in that vulnerability.

As we move across the room as one, you encounter yet another, a further point of contact, an additional invitation to new dynamics of movement. An entirely new body, a unique way of moving, being, listening, initiating, following. You become the point of mediation between us three. Each dances their own rhythm with you; polyphonic you become. Your shoulder moves in a different tempo than your hip, accommodating both within your body, which itself takes on a new fluidity in the challenge of mediation. Another joins: a group concresces at various points of contact and becomes one body with many limbs — a mini body politic. Movements of each reverberate across all; your expressions directly influence the larger whole. You are amplified. Your arm, through the extension of many bodies, reaches across to the far side of the room. A moving bundle. Where do we go from here? Our goal is to decide by all listening to what is needed and trying something out. You move, I follow; I move, you follow. No one moves. We all head for different directions. We fall apart, too many separate agendas, and we learn to find one another again or decide that it is better to go our own ways. We discover in the process how often and how dramatically each decides to shift our course, how to take turns guiding, each individually noting when one steers and how one let's oneself be steered, and then examining why.

Our dancing here is not structured around a fixed choreographic script that shapes movement in specific directions; our aim is not the production of an aesthetic nor is it only to engage with the material forces at work in our movement. In dancing together on the basis of physical contact, which involves sharing in each other's embodiment, movement patterns, and the physical forces that shape our connection, we enter into an ethical relationship to one another, an ethical relationship premised on equal respect for one another's agency, care, support, and the attention and self-reflection that this requires. The choreography primarily at work here is heightened listening and maximally generous responsiveness. Gestures are responses to the questions "what do you need from my movement?", "how do I hold your weight with spacious softness as you twist around me?", and "how can my body offer your body a pathway of support while you try to balance?" We come to the practice on the basis of an ethic, and further discover the meaning and nuances of this ethic through the practice. Some dancers are more experienced, but not because they have mastered a ready-made vocabulary; it is because they have unfolded their ability to perceive and have learned the ease of movement through practice. We have all been beginners, and in an art based on improvisation we are beginners ever anew.

We set the agenda together. And we figure out what that means by trying to do so. Which movements allow for mutuality in decision-making around where to move? Which do not? If I move too quickly, you become unsure of where I am, and I lose you. If I move too slowly, you become unsure of where I am, and I lose you. If I move with unacknowledged aggression, you may become scared, and I lose you. Equal participation in guiding a movement depends on and is a result, an achievement, of a process of mutual calibration over time. I am lighter than you thought; you are more excitable than I thought. We adjust to find each other and evolve in the process. Without sufficient exploration of and experimentation with one another's subtleties, we cannot hope to become equal participants in a shared creation here or elsewhere.

The lean was too hard, I was too tense, so I couldn't support your weight, and fell out of our balance, you tumbling with me; on the floor we renegotiate and recalibrate our understanding of what each other's capabilities are, without blaming ourselves or one another — or noting our impulse to blame and putting a question mark around it. We attend to failure, to the misunderstandings in which it is sourced, and fine-tune our perceptions in its light. Sometimes we aren't sure how or whether to start again. We sit in the blockage until something new emerges, until we are ready to begin again, or to recalibrate on our own or with others.

Is this sensibility not what we aim for in a democracy? Would not our capacities to be democratic subjects be supported if we had cultural sites wherein we could actively experiment with not just leading or following, but with co-deciding in action and playfully exploring our agency? Would this not take profound root in us if this cultural site involved the intelligence of our sensitive, emotional bodies?

THINK FUTURE, ACT PRESENT: DREAMS OF CREATIVE DEMOCRACIES

LÁSZLÓ UPOR

Carry That Weight[1]

A legendary Hungarian professor of dentistry begins his new course each year by warning the students: "Note that the tooth you are treating always ends in a human." Whether the story is true or not is of minor importance because it teaches a simple but important lesson about parts and *the whole*, about organs and organisms.

You cannot "cure" a decayed democracy as an abstract idea (or fill the cavities), while ignoring the people involved. The human element. Body and mind; flesh, blood, nerves. Social tissue. And social movements are among the most effective treatments to repair and regenerate this particular tissue: the vital and highly sensitive organ of our body politic.

More than a protest, less than a revolution (although possibly a descendant of the first and the ancestor of the second), a movement may fight for a cause not for power. Progressive movements will, however,

---

[1] All of the subheads in this essay are borrowed from titles of Beatles songs, primarily from the 1969 album *Abbey Road*.

change attitudes and *transform the power structures* eventually. The accumulated effect of these movements is the construction of the anteroom to a more civil-friendly hall of democracy.

Social movements are not necessarily about *big numbers*, not about the mass: their strength derives from the collaboration of devoted people through collective action.

Golden Slumbers

Collective action shall wake up the individual and groups of individuals from their long sleep, whether in creepy corners of freezing shelters or in comfortable king-size beds in cozy homes. Collective action must rip the windows of Sleeping Beauty's castle open — let the fresh air in and remind people of the power of the (individual and collective) self as well as of their responsibilities.

Collective action is to a society as practicing is to musicians or dancers. Artists need talents and activists need ideas. But none can perform without the *everyday routine* of exhausting and demanding practice. And there is no sabbatical.

Collective action will not solve the ultimate problems of our race: it is not the famous sword of Alexander the Great that cuts through the Gordian knot of the global polycrisis, but it may help the Global Polis to *find ways* and gradually untie that knot through common effort.

Collective action may not save the world but it can train and prepare communities that eventually *will*, by stimulating the collective mind, evaporating cynicism, heating up frozen solidarity, and cooling down boiling hatred. Train and flex the muscles of the *true* body politic.

Maxwell's Silver Hammer

Collective action is not an end in itself but multidimensional research, a learning process, constant trial and error, an ever-unfinished business, an exercise in forms of communication and exchange. While working on a common task, individuals experience and realize how their contribution changes the course of matters *in general* — and how collective collaborative action (different from the mob-like "togetherness"!) may become one strong pillar of a future society.

Collective action is a multifunctional liberation tool (DIY!) that serves, partly, to dismantle hierarchies and erase privileges, and ease the distrust, frustration, and embarrassment of the disempowered. More than a valuable *side effect*, this is an integral part of the long-term plan. At its best, collective action disarms the powerful and arms the powerless. Helps people trust each other (again) and believe in the meaning and possibility of action. By doing you prove *it is possible*. By doing you challenge the paralyzing fear and doubt (imposed by the arrogance of oppressive rulers and institutions). Collective action is best to nurture courage and boost morale. Fighting for a cause while negotiating, developing, and fine-tuning each other's ideas, by actively participating in formulating the common will and executing the plan, creates and builds community.

Collective action: always a question mark or an exclamation mark — never a full stop. A movement is the opposite of stasis — and this is not just a play on words. Don't let the system freeze. Keep it on alert.

Collective action may be a response to despair but can only be effective if it is inspired and conducted by the fearless and responsive imagination of the involved.

A movement may need leaders and definitely needs a *vision*, but it is never about one leader, or a one-person *mission* with many followers. The rise of individualism is the death of a movement — there are examples galore.

Something

The future of democracy lies in the present: it is guaranteed only by the presence of the present democracy (or: without its presence in the present, it's a lost cause). You must not sacrifice, suspend, or postpone basic democratic values today in order to build *tomorrow's democracy* (that is not to say that sacrifices may not be necessary). "Oh, I am all for democracy *in principle*, but need to implement undemocratic practices *temporarily* to be effective in building our democratic future." There is no such thing as the future of democracy if you don't believe in the possibility of potent democracy in the present. Time and space are inseparable, so why don't we paraphrase the slogan "think global, act local" as *think future, act present*.

Raise awareness, organize, act. Participate, invite, analyze, reorganize, refine, redirect. Resist, stand up, speak up. Act. Together. Embrace. Feed and get fed on each other's experience. Learn from the previous generation, teach the next generation.

Because

We proudly adapt. That is one of our signature characteristics. The species homo sapiens, with its sophisticated physical-chemical-biological-spiritual system, is highly adaptable to slowly changing conditions — even to those we shouldn't stand. Not only our bodies but our minds are dressed to accommodate. With obvious benefits. But.

The political climate crisis of our times is only comparable to the meteorological climate crisis. Growing gaps in living conditions, an unprecedented concentration of power and wealth, overwhelming propaganda (a state-of-the-art brainwashing machine), the victorious march of the non-fact, a growing realm of post truth. Plus, a wide range of (anti) social phobias, shamelessly used and abused by politicians and fueled and pumped-up by the media. Still, we adapt and adapt again, potentially to our own detriment, like those doomed mythical frogs in a pot of water slowly coming to a boil. Partly because we train ourselves to ignore the early signs and only react with a deadly delay, partly because we chose to respond individually. But collective action can help the individual and the smaller units of society recognize the dangerous rising temperature of our semi-comfortable society — and turn down the heat or knock over the pot of boiling water in time.

Come Together

A long history of political actions and movements prove how important the *joy of acting together* is to the success of a movement. Centuries — and especially the last decades — produced spectacular examples of festive resistance. Activists and their collaborating partners, participants, and audiences (that is, potential future collaborators) need and deserve the feeling of community manifested in (and fueled by) shared laughter. And in the joy of creating. Creating something unexpected, something that holds. Images, sounds. Visual, acoustic, and spiritual signs. Slogans. Symbols.

Just how important those reminders are is evident in how major achievements by the superstars or everyday heroes of science, art, and activism are recognized and referred to. Big moments burn a lasting image into our minds and souls. Some are imprints, traces of a past or ongoing process, others are created in advance to identify something still shifting and shaping. Ordinary objects are reframed in new contexts, everyday actions find new meanings, common locations become places of pilgrimage, while others are *born symbols*.

The ubiquitous number Pi, Mona Lisa's mysterious smile, Picasso's shorts, and Glenn Gould's famously low piano chair; "the" zebra crossing on Abbey Road, Neil Armstrong's footprint on the Moon, Ruby Bridges' first steps into a desegregated school in New Orleans in 1960, Mahatma Gandhi's 240-mile Salt March in 1930, and giant puppet "refugee" Little Amal's travels (*The Walk*) across the seven seas in search of her mother and a new home; Maria Skłodowska's (aka Marie Curie's) *second* Nobel Prize, Greta Thunberg's "Fridays for Future," and Patti Smith's embarrassing but utterly human slip-up at the 2016 Nobel Ceremony; Stonewall Inn in New York, Tiananmen Square in Beijing, Maidan in Kyiv, and the Gezi Park in Istanbul; "I Have a Dream," Black Lives Matter, "Nothing About Us Without Us," and Woman, Life, Freedom. None of this needs further explanation.

We long for images, symbols (colors, visual patterns), music, and slogans on the threshold of the material and the spiritual, to relate to. To identify with. To translate, convey, and pinpoint high concepts. To encourage others to join the community and contribute, first just by sharing and actively using the symbols. Symbols have their own lives. They live much longer than the actions and movements that created them. They get revisited, recycled, reinterpreted, revived, adapted. Integrated. Refined. Developed.

Movements learn from each other, borrow methods, tools, ideas, ideals (sometimes even idealists) from their predecessors or sibling-movements. This is part of their strength; this is how the smallest-size and the shortest-living ones may be as influential as their stronger, bigger fellow-movements.

Here Comes the Sun

We don't know what a future democracy will look like. We don't know much about the future of democracy — therefore pre-planned scholarly research is not enough: we need to *actively experiment*. The way scientists do, the way artists do. The future of democracy may not lie in our strong belief in one *particular democracy* but in an endless experiment with *democracies*. (No, not the constant shifting and bending of principles the way autocrats do. And no, not appealing to the lowest common denominator the way populists do. Populism is the travesty of "power to the people".) Social movements are institutions of advanced studies in (participatory) democracy.

A true laboratory for democracy is the realm of social movements (thus, social movements are laboratories for democracy): a learning society composed of various fields of study where the possibility of making errors is part of the deal. The power of being able to correct mistakes reinforces the belief in change and the flexibility of the complex system. Complex problems need complex solutions: not just a *social dentist* but a team of specialists and health workers to tend to *the whole body*.

Complexity needs imagination. In mathematics an imaginary (that is, "not real") number (i) can, by filling a cavity, extend the *real number* system to the *complex number* system — which is very real indeed.

Collective action — group activism fueled by arts and sciences — does just that: fills the gap (or builds a bridge) between known realities. Paints a bright sky above the monochrome political ideologies and dictates of grim, numbing reality. Collective action must break the plaster sarcophagus of harmful dichotomies that — when solidified — fatally separates people from each other, thus paralyzing both the individual and the society. Collective action is Einstein sticking out his tongue.

With modern science — new geometry, quantum physics, psychoanalysis and more — we lost the firm ground of a previously coherent world view but gained a whole new universe to explore and inhabit. We learned how non-Euclidean geometries, with their surprising *parallel postulates*, reformed modern natural science and made (among other things) space travel possible. We haven't yet worked out, however, what *non-Euclidean society* will look like if we revise the *participatory democracy postulate*.

You don't need to be an artist or a researcher to be part of, or even initiate, a movement, but if you are an artist or/and a researcher, then you'd better take part in social movements.

Octopus's Garden

Art and science must descend from the ivory tower. The tower may — and sometimes must — provide a safe and quiet environment to test and nurture high ideas in soundproof laboratories. But neither science nor art should lock themselves up permanently in the secluded and padded top chambers of that tower.

You may work in your Sacred Ivory Tower and still reside in the village — while using the sky-high ladder, the light-speed escalator, a number of multicolor musical inflated slides, laser beams, or the rainbow parachute and a magic balloon of imagination to travel up and down between the two.

Descend from the ivory tower (a good place to observe the stars) to ground level and below, into the deep seas, where you can navigate with amazement the labyrinth of the laboratory of life. Find inspiration in analyzing the simple complexity of a protozoon, in observing the incredible octopus with its three hearts and all-over mysterious brain. The highly impossible axolotl and the unimaginable sea slug, with its capacity to decapitate itself to survive. See how it preserves its autonomy through autotomy when the worst comes to worst.

Study the coexistence, the symbioses, the rich connections within the all-global system. No organism is too simple, none is too complicated, if you look with curiosity and compassion. Raise a celebratory glass to the invitational, collaborative nature of creation.

And, when toasting, think of the multifaceted cooperation of human and non-human in creating the wine you have in your glass. First mineral, plant, soil, weed, insects, bees, sun, wind, and rain (possibly snow and ice); then fungi, steel tanks, oak barrels and amphorae, temperature, and humidity; later bottles and corks; eventually air again — your vision, your nose and taste buds to absorb the acids, sugars, a wide spectrum of smell and taste. Imperceptible is the visible change of the separate contributing elements — still, their accumulative contribution is immense and produces something unique.

Just the way the individual's creative spirit adds a distinct flavor to the collective action without losing the self. Again, and again, and again.

Here, there, and everywhere.

Across the universe.

ABOUT THE AUTHORS

Madhulika Banerjee is a Professor in the Department of Political Science at the University of Delhi.

Michael Brüggemann is Professor of Communication Research, Climate and Science Communication at the University of Hamburg.

John Aubrey Douglass is a Senior Research Fellow and Research Professor in Public Policy and Higher Education at the University of California, Berkeley.

Isabel Feichtner is Professor of Public Law and International Economic Law at the University of Würzburg.

Frederic Hanusch is Interim Professor of Planetary Change and Politics at Justus Liebig University Giessen and co-founder of its Panel on Planetary Thinking.

Anna Katsman is the Academic Director of THE NEW INSTITUTE.

Louis J. Kotzé is a Research Professor of Law at North-West University, South Africa.

Max Krahé is co-founder and Research Director of Dezernat Zukunft.

Bruno Leipold is a Fellow in Political Theory at the London School of Economics and Political Science.

Tobias Müller is a Leverhulme Early Career Fellow at the Centre for Research in the Arts, Social Sciences and Humanities (CRASSH) at the University of Cambridge.

Minna Salami is a Nigerian-Finnish and Swedish feminist author and social critic.

Maki Sato is a Project Associate Professor at the University of Tokyo, East Asian Academy for New Liberal Arts.

Judith Simon is Professor for Ethics in Information Technology at the University of Hamburg.

Rahel Süß is a Fellow at the urban democracy project "The Esch Clinics" at the University of Luxembourg.

Ece Temelkuran is a novelist, political thinker, and investigative journalist.

László Upor is a dramaturg, literary translator, professor, and founding member of the Freeszfe Society, formed by students and faculty who left SzFE (University of Theatre and Film Arts, Budapest).

Andrej Zwitter is Professor of Political Theory, Chair of Governance and Innovation and co-founder of the inter- and transdisciplinary branch Faculty Campus Fryslân at the University of Groningen.

ABOUT THE ILLUSTRATIONS

MAC PREMO[1]

Collage as a medium eliminates its own author. The artist relinquishes total control and embarks on an agreement to democratize communication and knowledge. I borrow images, reassign and realign them, and they take on new meaning. But that new meaning could never exist without relying on the shared meaning of the initial imagery. The elements of collage have a very important job: they provide context. From there, messaging is created in alliance with the contextual worldview established by that imagery; collage is always a conversation, never a declaration.

 These images were created through a mix of analog and digital collage. Each construction of found imagery, texture, and color-field was arranged atop a light table. The camera was locked off in a fixed position, and each composition was photographed with multiple exposures and with a mixture of illumination setups: some completely backlit through the light table, some lit completely from above, and some with a mixture of lighting. Additionally, several translucent colored plexiglass plates were laid over each arrangement. The final illustrations were created by combining

1 Mac Premo is an artist and filmmaker based in New York. He was involved in several programs as a fellow at THE NEW INSTITUTE in 2023–24.

these analogue layers of varying opacity as digital layers. Ultimately, these illustrations are the result of single compositions photographed at different times and in different conditions but presented as a single moment in this book. The intention is to bring a sense of temporality to the imagery, as they reflect conditions that are not static, but alive and transpiring.

Collages are inherently democratic. They rely on ideas that already exist, that have already been built and formed — collage seeks to reshape these concepts to forge new meaning. The new idea is a construction of existing concepts, rearranged and reconfigured, that creates a new vantage point. This new image is composed of elements from contributors, not arbiters, and the composition of the final piece relies on the strength of the gathered building materials. If we're going to get anywhere, it's going to be through a process of (re)imagining.

ACKNOWLEDGEMENTS

We extend our sincere gratitude to three anonymous reviewers whose valuable feedback and suggestions significantly strengthened this volume. Their expertise was invaluable in shaping the final manuscript. We appreciate the time and effort they invested in improving *Seeds for Democratic Futures*. Diana's tireless work as Editorial Manager was instrumental in coordinating the various stages of production, ensuring that each aspect of the process ran smoothly and efficiently, and her dedication greatly contributed to the successful completion of this project.